WORKING
WITH
LEATHER

WORKING WITH LEATHER

Xenia Ley Parker

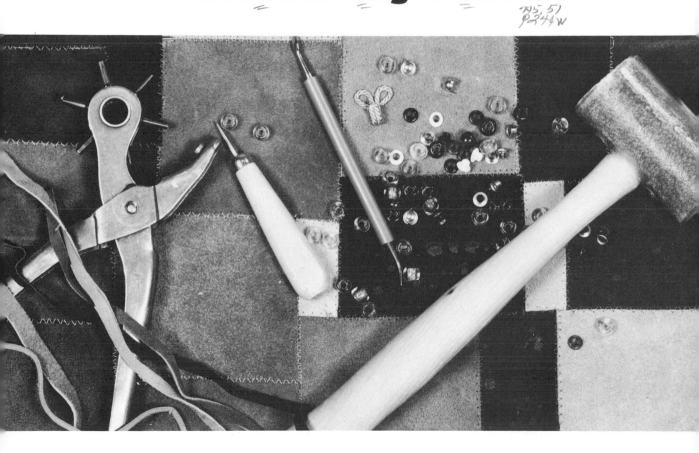

Charles Scribner's Sons   New York

Line drawings by Olga Ley
Color photographs by Paulin-Gilmore Studios

Printed in the United States of America
Library of Congress Catalog Card Number 77-37227
SBN 684-12760-1 (Trade cloth)

To Martin

I wish to express my thanks to all those who have made this book possible and especially to Barthold Fles, Nancy Greenberg, and my editor, Elinor Parker.

CONTENTS

FOREWORD

THE NEW LEATHERCRAFTER

In today's world of mass production techniques, there are a growing number of people who favor the individuality of hand-crafted clothing and accessories. This appreciation is increasingly evident all around us as more new artisans design, make and wear the products of their own creativity. These new craftsmen and women aren't much interested in turning out bookmarks and penwipers as a hobby—they're eager to put their time to more meaningful use. This book can show them how.

Leather lends itself well to this feeling of self-expression and practicality. The supple beauty of the material is only part of the enjoyment; leather is fun to work with and easy to handle. Furthermore, it's possible to make suede and leather articles for a fraction of their comparable retail cost.

The results can be truly delightful.

CHAPTER ONE

Leather
Then and Now

The earliest inhabitants of this planet discovered that animal skins were more practical to wear than to eat. It was a question of durability; aesthetic admiration was yet to come.

Man's first real garments consisted of raw hides roughly tied around the wearer's body. Later, during the Stone Age, bone tools were utilized to clean and sew pelts into crude clothing. However, it was untanned and not quite leather as we know it.

The origins of tanning are obscure, but the ancient Hebrews are known to have devised an oak bark process that is still in use today. There are numerous references to leather in the Old Testament which help establish its place in recorded history. It was an important trade commodity throughout the cradle of civilization. The sea-faring Phoenicians spread the colorful influence of Babylonian embroidered and decorated leatherwork to other Mediterranean countries. Their reddish-purple dyes, derived from the insect *kermes*, were so distinctive that the color was known as Phoenician Red.

Egyptian shoes and other artifacts found in the tombs of Pharaohs were in surprisingly good condition, their red, green, purple, white and natural brown leathers having lasted for literally thousands of years.

The first recorded tanner's guild appeared during the early days of the Roman Empire. The tongued buckle, much as we know it today, was introduced around the same time and gained immediate popularity on belts and other articles. The craftmanship of sandals and boots was so important that their quality made the status of the owner readily apparent to everyone. Anyone visiting modern Rome will note the longevity of this custom.

The legions of Rome prized leather for its protective qualities. The soldiers made wide use of it as body armor in the form of breast plates, tunics and shields.

When the Roman armies invaded the cold north of Europe they found the nomadic Teutonic tribes fully dressed for the weather, with leather forming an integral part of their wardrobe. On their eventual return to Rome, many soldiers shocked their togaed countrymen with their adoption of the barbaric custom of wearing leather pants, called braccae. The Emperor went so far as to ban the wearing of these first trousers within city limits, but to no avail. Sooner or later, men everywhere were won over to the new style.

In Medieval Europe the most coveted leather was known as Cordovan, Cordwain or, simply, Spanish Leather. It was made in Cordoba,

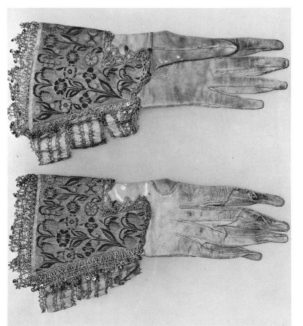

The Metropolitan Museum of Art, gift of Edward S. Harkness, 1928

Buff leather gloves with tapestry cuffs. English, late 16th century

Sandalled workers in old Pompeii (a reconstruction by F. Matania)

Spain, by the conquering Moors, who had brought the secret of its manufacture from their homeland. The softly tanned goatskin was dyed in many colors and often perfumed for ladies' wear. It was imported from Spain in vast quantities until other countries later developed similar tanning methods.

By the time of the Renaissance, tanners' guilds were in existence all over Europe. Leather was used for gloves, boots, shoes, purses, belts, vests called jerkins, and jackets, or doublets. The Moors, having been driven from Spain, set up the new quarters for their work in Morocco, which probably explains why goatskin is still referred to as Moroccan Leather, even when it is made elsewhere.

Half a world away, the Mayan, Incan and Aztec civilizations of Central and South America were quite advanced in the art of tanning and creating leather articles, as reported by the first explorers.

When Europeans arrived in North America, they found Indians wearing clothing made of lovely yellow, red and white buckskin, deerskin or buffalo hide. The Indians made good use of all parts of the animals they hunted, creating food, clothing, shelter, transportation and tools.

Frontier suit c. 1780

Valentine Museum, Richmond, Virginia

14

Leather was made by the women of the tribe and due to geographical separation, each group had its own particular method of tanning.

As colonists settled in the New World, they learned the Indian way of oil tanning and added it to the knowledge they brought with them from Europe. By the end of the seventeenth century, there were tanneries throughout the colonies.

A hundred years later, a break-through was made with the discovery that oak bark was not the only plant derivative that could be used for tanning. Extracts from other plants were found to be equally effective, including the bark of hemlock and chestnut trees, which grew in abundance in North America.

The frontiersmen adopted many Indian-style garments for comfort and protection during the hazardous exploration and settlement of the American West. They wore a great deal of leather, mainly buffalo hide or buckskin fringed jackets and vests, chaps or open sided pants, gloves, gauntlets and boots. Even their hats were trimmed with tooled leather bands.

During the nineteenth century there were many advances made in the art of leather manufacture, as there were in all industries. An American chemist invented a tanning method using chromium salts that took a few hours instead of the weeks or months required for vegetable tanning. Machines were developed that cut the time needed to make leather even further. Since many operations were no longer done by hand, production became less tedious and more economical.

Today's leather is made with many steps of cleaning and soaking in preparation for tanning. After these processes, the skins are sorted, graded and split into varying thicknesses by machine. Some skins are selected for sueding, where the flesh side of the skin is buffed to produce its characteristic pile. Tanning then proceeds, with either chemical or vegetable tans being chosen according to the type of leather desired. Then the skins are washed, pressed and polished. Certain skins are oiled, greased or waxed. Others are dyed in many colors, usually with coal tar or aniline dyes and then finished.

Modern American leathers are constantly being improved, as new finishes and colors are created. The richness and variety of leathers available to everyone at reasonable prices would be the envy of ancient potentates.

CHAPTER TWO

Leathers and Suedes— and How to Buy

One of the most pleasant surprises in store for the new leather buyer is the wide variety of suedes and leathers available. Each type is suited to a range of uses, according to its unique characteristics. Choosing the right one for the job is easy, once you know what to look for.

The names of leathers themselves are fairly descriptive. The suffixes, hide and skin, tell the relative size of the animal; hides are from large animals as in cowhide and steerhide, skins are from smaller animals such as calfskin or sheepskin. A kip is a small hide. The hair or outer side of the skin is called the grain side and the inner, the flesh side.

Leather is tanned and finished so that the grain side has a smooth rich surface. A brief description of the most common types of leather follows:

CALFSKIN—very fine grain, from the skins of young cows; comes in all colors and natural tan

COWHIDE—thick, strong, smooth finish; natural tan and a few shades

DOESKIN—fine and light, usually lamb or sheepskin; many colors; washable

ELKHIDE—heavy, now made from cowhide tanned to look like elk; natural tan and brown

KIDSKIN—many finishes, made of goatskin; all colors

LAMBSKIN—often embossed with the grain of another animal such as ostrich or alligator or with a pattern that looks like tooled leather; some colors, usually brown or black

MOROCCO—fine, lovely finish, made of goatskin; thin but long wearing; comes in a limited number of colors and is especially known for its rich red hue

PIGSKIN—tough and durable with interesting grain; some colors; comparatively inexpensive

SHEEPSKIN—called Cabretta, smooth and pliant, from the haired sheep (wooly sheep do not produce leather); all colors.

SKIVER—thin, split skins of calf, sow or sheep; some colors; used mainly for linings

STEERHIDE—heavy and strong, crinkle grain finish; natural tan and some reds and browns, sometimes comes in two or three tone hides

Suede is made by roughening and buffing the flesh side of selected skins to create its nap or pile finish. The process was first developed in Sweden and named Suede, or Swedish, by the French. Today many animal skins are sueded, the most popular being described below:

ANTELOPE—very fine, lightweight, lovely texture; many colors; expensive and sometimes hard to find

BUCKSKIN—strong, soft and durable, made of sheep or calfskin now, originally buck or deerskin; some colors, usually white, beige, yellow and red; water resistant

CHAMOIS—lightweight, strong, made of split sheep or calfskin; characteristic soft yellow color; washable and well known for its cleaning abilities, gaining popularity for use in clothing

LAMBSKIN—called Garment Suede, the most easily available suede; comes in all colors, even tie-dyed

SHEEPSKIN—similar texture and appearance of lambskin; many colors

SPLIT COWHIDE—sometimes called Garment Split, strong, versatile and fast growing in popularity; available in many different weights and colors

SUEDED PIGSKIN—buffed on the grain side maintaining its interesting turf like grain; some colors; can be difficult to find

In choosing leather or suede for a project, careful consideration of the most suitable type is the basic step. The following charts depict the weights and sizes of the most popular craft leathers, with special attention to their appropriate usage.

CHARACTERISTICS OF SUEDES

TYPE	WEIGHT (per square foot)	SKIN SIZE (sq. feet)	USES
Antelope	2-3 ounces	5-9	Men's jackets, women's clothing
Buckskin	2-4	7-9	Jackets, vests, pants, coats
Chamois	2-3	7-9	Shirts, light clothing
Lambskin (Garment Suede)	2-3	5-7	Men's and women's clothing; skirts, jackets, pocket books, pillows, linings
Sheepskin	2-3	7-9	Like lambskin
Split Cowhide (Garment Split) Light		6-8	Versatile for men's and women's wear of all types; vests, jackets, ponchos, skirts, pants
Medium	3½-4	7-10	Clothing, belts, hats, coats, hand bags, tote bags
Sueded Pigskin	3-4	5-8	Purses, belts, wallets, key cases

18

CHARACTERISTICS OF LEATHERS

TYPE	WEIGHT (per square foot)	SKIN SIZE (sq. feet)	USES
Calfskin	3-4 ounces	12-15	Finest grain for tooling projects of all kinds
Cowhide Light	2-3½	18-25	Men's and women's wear; jackets, vests; upholstery
Medium	4-7	18-25	Easily carved and tooled; small projects, belts, wallets, hand bags, sandals
Heavy	8-10	16-20	Good for larger tooling projects; briefcases, pocketbooks, book cases
Doeskin	1-2	3-5	Mainly used for gloves; luxurious shirts
Goatskin (Morocco)	2-3	4-6	Dyes well; book bindings, belts, wallets, small articles
Kidskin	1-2	3-5	Durable linings, gloves, light vests, shirts
Pigskin	3-4	5-8	Hard wear items; purses, wallets, book bindings
Sheepskin (Cabretta)	2-3	5-9	Women's clothing; jackets, skirts, coats, vests
Steerhide	3-4	12-15	Large tooling projects; saddles, brief cases, suitcases

The use of exotic animal and reptile skins, once in plentiful supply, is undesirable because of the threat of extinction that endangers their original owners. Alligator, crocodile, lizard and ostrich skins, to name a few, have become increasingly rare. Excellent copies of these distinctive grains have been embossed on various leathers with good results. These skins are available at lesser cost to both the leathercrafter and the environment, and should serve equally well for any project that calls for an exotic skin.

Some snakeskins, notably Cobra and Python, come from snakes raised on farms specifically for this purpose and are in easy supply. Cobra is dyed many colors, particularly blues, greens, reds and browns. Python retains its lovely natural black or brown and white pattern. Both skins are thin but strong, and usually from 4 to 6 inches wide and 18 to 36 inches long. Although fairly expensive, snakeskins are great for small items or decorative application to larger leather or suede projects.

Now that you've chosen the kind of leather, suede or other skin you're looking for, you should know how to look for it.

Leather is sold by the skin, half skin or quarter skin. The price is calculated by the number of square feet in each skin. The skins are marked on the wrong side in quarter feet, with the numbers 1, 2 and 3 standing for, respectively, ¼, ½ and ¾ of a foot. For example, a skin marked 6³ would be 6 and ¾ feet square. Sometimes leather is sold pre-cut by the foot, like fabric, but this is probably the most expensive way to buy it. Since you can always save unused pieces, buying by the skin is more economical in the long run.

Skins should be thoroughly checked for weaknesses, marks and tears. All skins have a couple of minor defects, but if there are too many, those parts of the skin will be useless. Stains and imperfections cannot be removed, so be sure to look at what you're getting. Often, slightly damaged skins will be grouped together for sale at a lower price. These can be worth checking out, as they may contain enough usable leather to make them a real bargain.

Another thing to remember when buying a specific amount is that the edges and leg areas of the skin aren't the best quality, but can be used for linings and places that don't show. While buying a hide, estimate the best part as being around one foot smaller, for a skin one half foot smaller, than the total square footage.

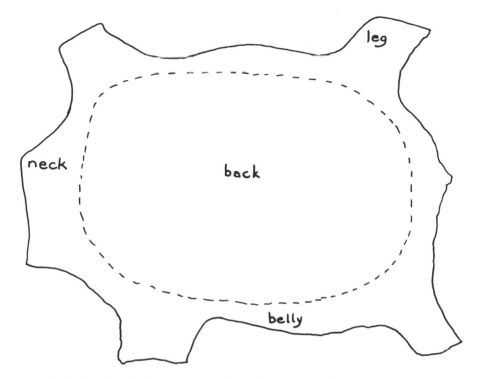

A typical skin with the best part of the leather outlined.

When purchasing several skins for several projects or larger items, ask about the quantity price beforehand. Most stores will give discounts that increase with the number of skins purchased. These savings customarily apply to leathers of the same kind, but can include different colors.

Bundles of odd pieces of leather are sold by the pound. Unfortunately, some packages have large pieces and others have only small scraps that aren't very useful. If there's an opportunity to examine one of these bundles before getting it, it may be a real buy, with pieces large enough to use for many articles.

Currently popular are kits of pre-cut leather containing everything needed to assemble various projects. The convenience is perhaps outweighed by the expense, considering the actual amount of leather you get. Besides, it's really much more exciting to choose your own patterns and leathers with the knowledge that the finished product will be an original.

Unused leather can be stored indefinitely with proper care. It should never be folded, as the creases along the fold will not come out. Ideally, leather should be laid out flat or draped over a padded surface. If space doesn't permit, it can be loosely rolled with the grain side out. Warning—if the grain side is rolled inward, it will wrinkle and the resulting lines can't be removed. Leather should also be kept in a dark place, since it fades if exposed to a bright light for a long time.

Finding a store that sells leather becomes easier all the time, as more and more people discover the joy of creative leatherwork. Look in the classified telephone book under Leather—Retail or Arts and Crafts Supplies. There are also many mail order companies that sell everything one could want. Their catalogues illustrate and describe the leathers and equipment available and help take the guesswork out of ordering by mail. One word of caution—the bundles of leather mentioned earlier are best not ordered by mail unless described as containing a specified number of large pieces.

CHAPTER THREE

The Tools of the Trade

There are a great many tools made just for the leather-crafter. They're all useful and fun to own; but it's fun to be economical too. For most articles, a surprisingly small number of tools can be used successfully.

A good basic group of tools for all early projects is:

A. SCISSORS—to cut leather. Any good, strong, sharp scissors can be used.

B. ALL PURPOSE LEATHER KNIFE—to cut and skive, or thin, leather.

C. ROTARY HOLE PUNCH—available with four or six different size tubes, to punch holes for lacing, rivet, eyelet and snap setting.

D. HAND GRIP EYELET SETTER—with attachments that are used to set eyelets, grommets and snap fasteners.

E. STITCH GAUGE—for correct marking and placement of hand stitches. This can be done with a ruler and pen, but the gauge is the most efficient method.

F. SHOEMAKER'S AWL—to pierce holes for hand sewing and

stud placement. Can be bought with exchangeable points of varying sizes.

G. AN L-SHAPED STEEL RULER—to measure, place and guide cutting of straight lines; mark and set up patterns and projects.

H. NEEDLES—of heavy weight specifically for leatherwork, the curved needle being for hard to reach places. Where stitches are pre-punched by an awl, any heavyweight needle can be used.

For special effects and more complicated work, this second group of tools can come in handy:

A. SKIVING KNIFE—specifically for thinning leather.

B. DRAW GAUGE KNIFE—to cut strips of heavy weight leather for belts and straps. Adjustable for widths from ¼ to 4 inches.

C. EDGE BEVELER—to trim the edges of leather. Comes in different sizes for various weight leathers.

D. MALLET—used in conjunction with other tools, usually made of wood or rolled rawhide. Any lightweight hammer will suffice, but craft mallets are the easiest to use.

E. ROUND DRIVE PUNCH—used with mallet to punch holes in places hard to reach with a hand-punch. Comes in sizes No. 00, the smallest, to No. 10, the largest.

F. OBLONG DRIVE PUNCH—to make slots in belts, bags, etc. Available in sizes from ½ to 1 inch wide.

G. EYELET SPREADER—used with mallet.

H. SNAP SETTER—also used with mallet, as E. and G., in places a hand-grip setter will not reach.

I. THONGING CHISEL—used with mallet to make slits for lacing. Available in one to four pronged models.

J. LACING NEEDLE—to ease laces through slits.

K. PLIERS—to aid in lacing and hand-sewing by pulling needle through tight places.

L. WIRE CUTTER—although not a leathercraft tool, a jeweler's wire cutter can be used to snip the edges of leather where scissors or knives are difficult to use.

M. GOUGER—to cut heavy leathers in preparation for folding by making a groove for the crease.

N. EDGE CREASER—used to make a crease for sewing stitches to rest in or any decorative edge lines.

24

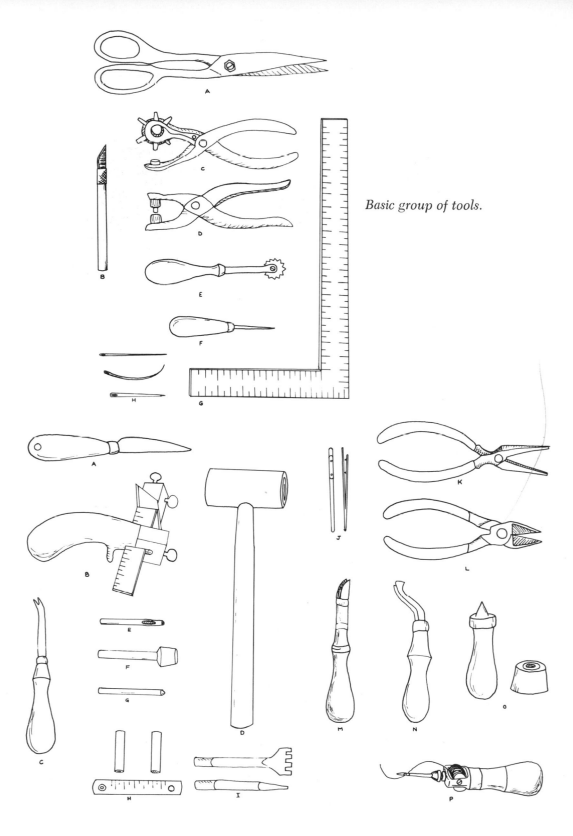

Basic group of tools.

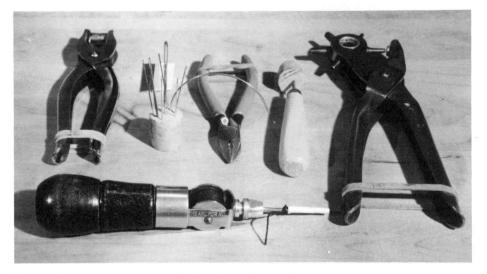

The right way to prepare tools for storage.

O. GROMMET SETTER—to set grommets into leather.

P. SEWING AWL—for hand-sewing.

When not in use, keep tools in a rack, box or drawer where they won't be damaged by contact with each other. Put sharp tools away most carefully, being sure that their edges are protected and won't hurt anyone. To keep cutting tools sharp and efficient, get an oilstone and follow the directions for its use. If stored and handled correctly, there will be little need to sharpen punches, awls and other such items.

For good results, a usable work space is a must. Room to lay out leather and equipment can be made on any table or surface. Hard wood or marble tops are excellent to work on and can be covered with a heavy sheet of plastic to protect the finish.

For cutting leather with a knife, you'll need a large piece of cardboard, linoleum or hard rubber, to be used as a cutting board. Soft wood may also be used, but the knife will have a tendency to follow the grain of the wood instead of your wishes.

Some type of cement is another necessity for successful leatherwork. Although there are special leather cements on the market, ordinary rubber cement can easily do the job. The brush in the lid of the jar is useful, and a quart can of cement can be used to refill the original jar when it is empty. This is the most economical way to use rubber cement. If the cement thickens, it loses its strength, so keep some cement thinner handy, and use it when needed. (Remember that the thinner is extremely flammable and take proper precautions.) Small squares of rubber, called cement pick-ups, are great to clean up the work area and are available in stationery stores, as is the cement thinner.

For marking patterns and placement of holes for snaps and other attachments, a soft lead pencil, ball-point pen or felt-tip pen can be used. Marking is almost always done on the underneath side of the skin, so any pen that gives a clear line is usable, since you don't have to worry about its showing on the finished piece of work. Dressmaker's chalk can be used when the right side of the leather must be marked, as it produces a light line that can be brushed off after cutting if it remains in view.

An extremely useful aid in making leather garments is an ordinary sewing machine. It can be readily adapted for use on lightweight leathers with a few simple attachments, and will be fully described in the chapter on sewing. However, this is a luxury that is not essential, as many of the most lovely articles made of leather are sewn or laced by hand.

Leather tooling and carving require special tools, discussed in Chapter Nine, which is devoted to this subject.

CHAPTER FOUR

How to Use Patterns

It's not hard to imagine the problems that would pop up if you started to build a house without first making some basic plans; it's the same with leather work. Well made leather articles, large or small, generally require the use of a pattern. A good pattern will answer many questions of fit and design before they can give you trouble and so allows you to work with a minimum of effort and material waste.

MAKING A PATTERN FROM AN EXISTENT OBJECT:

You can make your own patterns for most leather articles by copying them from things you already own or adapting them from the designs in this book. Your first pattern and project should be a simple one. As your skills grow, the complexity of the articles you'll want to make will naturally increase.

To start with; take some familiar object already on hand, such as a wallet, coin purse, belt, book jacket, portfolio, etc. and study its construction. Notice where and how it's sewn or fastened, how many separate pieces make up its construction—in short, how it was put together.

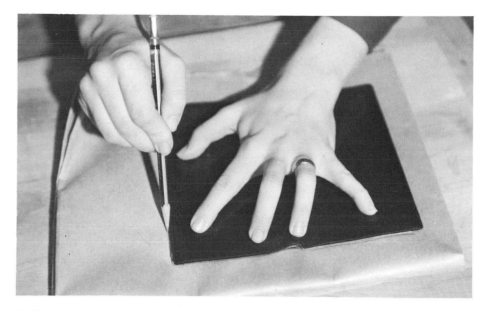

Making a pattern from an existent object.

Measure and write down the length and width of each part and then draw the parts on paper as you have measured them. Now, depending on the weight of the leather, add a one-eighth to one-quarter inch border to the edges of your drawing wherever a seam will occur; this allows room for sewing. If later you have to fold or crease the leather, allow for this in your drawing by adding two times the thickness of the leather to be used to the edges of the piece to be folded. After drawing your pattern, check its size and proportion by cutting out the paper pieces and fitting them over the corresponding parts of the original object.

If you've made your drawing carefully, the paper parts will be the same shape as the original and slightly larger in size to allow for seams and folds. For greater accuracy of design you can lightly assemble the paper parts using small pieces of tape that can be removed or cut away. After you're satisfied as to the size and shape of your paper pattern, glue the separated pieces to a thin piece of cardboard and cut them out, using household or paper scissors. Mark each piece as it's cut out, i.e. back of handbag, strap, flap etc. This will make the pattern easier to work with later on.

When first using this method of pattern making, start with an object that has only a few pieces and isn't too detailed or complicated. Also, when cutting any paper or cardboard pattern, try to use a pair of scissors other than the ones you'll be using on your leather. Paper can dull the cutting edges and sharp tools make leatherwork more enjoyable.

ORIGINAL PATTERNS:

Creating original patterns isn't as difficult as it sounds when you combine basic plans and your own individuality. It all adds up to a one of a kind design, and it's fun too.

Start with variations in size and shape applied to a basic design. For example, the handbag design as illustrated in Chapter Ten could be elongated, shortened, made round or oblong, more squared at the edges or flap, the strap changed and so on. Look at what's being displayed in stores or in magazines and books, adapt designs according to your own taste and need. Use a basic pattern as described and add, subtract or alter it completely. When you've acquired the feel of working with patterns, you'll probably want to make all kinds of unique and personal designs.

The principles of drawing, cutting and measurement are the same for original patterns as those used when making patterns from an existent object. You can draw the pattern directly onto cardboard if you prefer and eliminate the paper step after the method becomes familiar to you. If you intend to use the pattern many times over, it can be cut from heavier cardboard, sheet plastic or aluminum.

The possibilities for original patterns and projects are all around, just use your imagination and adapt what you like.

MARKING AND CUTTING A PATTERN ON LEATHER:

Put the prepared cardboard pattern on the inside of the leather so that marks will not show when the project is completed. Arrange the pattern pieces in a way that makes best use of the skin or hide. Check the outside of the leather to make certain that you're not including defects or blemishes that will mar the finished product's appearance. The edges

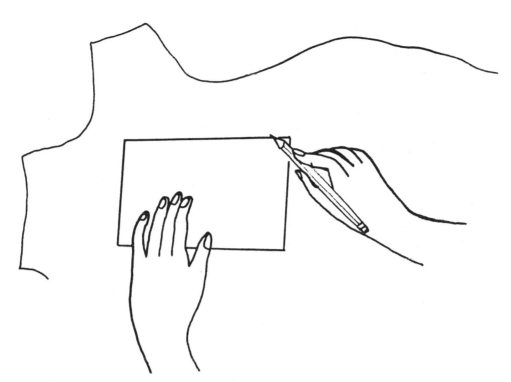

Outlining a pattern piece on a skin.

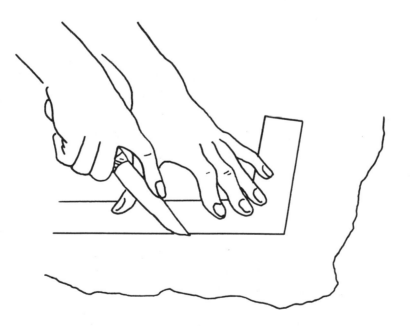

Cutting with a knife using an L shape ruler as a guide.

and leg areas of the skin, where imperfections are most evident, can be used for linings or hidden parts of the article.

Hold the cardboard piece firmly and trace its outline onto the leather using a ballpoint pen, felt-tip marker or soft lead pencil.

When all the project parts have been carefully outlined, the leather is ready for cutting.

Place the leather—still wrong side up—on a piece of heavy cardboard, linoleum or hard rubber working surface if you intend to make cuts with a craft or leather knife. Hold the knife at a forty-five degree angle and cut smoothly and steadily through the leather to the working surface beneath. If the cut isn't clean through the first time, repeat the process by following precisely in the same groove left by the first cut.

For straight lines, use a metal straight or L shaped ruler as a handy guide for the blade of the knife.

To cut a curved line for the first time, first practice a few cuts on a piece of scrap leather of the same weight to be used. Press firmly on the knife and draw the blade smoothly along the marked outline. Hold the leather in place to avoid snags that can result in an uneven or ragged edge. Cutting through to the cardboard, linoleum or hard rubber work surface helps to keep the blade steady for a cleaner cut. Wood surfaces tend to catch the point of the knife according to the grain of the wood and can alter its direction.

To cut leather using a sharp scissor or leather shear, use slow firm pressure to assure even edges. If cutting seems difficult, check to make certain that the scissor is really sharp. Dull blades are the most frequent cause of problems that occur when cutting light and medium-weight leather with shears. Another cause of difficult cutting may be the thickness of the leather. This can happen with the heavyweight hides, so match the tool to the job at hand.

LININGS:

You may wish to line some projects to add durability or for appearance. Some good lining materials to use are skivers, or thin splits of leather, garment suede or any lightweight skin that's not too expensive. Cloth linings are most frequently used in leather wearing apparel.

Linings should be cut either the same size as the project pieces or made a little larger and trimmed after they have been cemented in place. Remember to outline all parts on the wrong side of the lining leather, the part that won't show. Use a ballpoint pen or pencil as a marking felt pen may seep through the thin leather and stain it.

Cut the outlined parts from the thin leather just as you did the body of the project. Use a scissor or shears since the lightweight skin is so easy to cut. Of course, you can use a leather knife if you prefer. Whatever is most comfortable for you while getting the job done enjoyably and well is just what should be used.

If the article to be lined is to be sewn or laced, the lining should be attached after any necessary skiving—as described in chapters five and six—but before sewing or hole punching.

To attach a lining, put the leather for the lining and the project wrong side up on the work area. Cover the project leather completely with a thin coat of rubber cement. Apply the cement quickly with a brush. If the lining is the exact size, line up both pieces of leather at one edge and press the rest into place. Be sure to smooth out the lining while the glue is still wet to remove any lingering air pockets. If any cement seeps out between the two joined pieces, leave it alone. When it's completely dry you can roll any excess off with a bit of scrap leather or a cement pick-up. Don't try to remove the cement while it's even a little wet—it will never come off clean if you do. If too much cement oozes out of your work, use less, a little spreads a long way.

If the lining piece is larger follow the same procedure and trim the edges when the glue has completely dried. You can cut away the excess using scissors, a knife, or for tight places, jewelry wire cutters like those in Chapter Three.

To cement a lining to a folding part of an article, a slightly different procedure is followed. When the fold occurs in heavy leather, a groove should be cut into the flesh side of the leather where the fold will be. This is also true for heavy leather unlined articles too. Mark a line on the flesh side with a ruler and pen. Then using a gouger, cut along this line. There are two types of gouger, one, as illustrated in Chapter Three, is held in the hand. The other, illustrated here, is larger and rests on the leather as it is pushed along. A groove of this kind can also be made with a leather knife. Mark two lines, one on each side of the fold about an eighth of an inch apart. Cut a groove by first following one line and

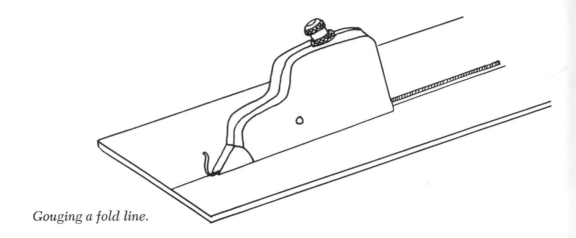

Gouging a fold line.

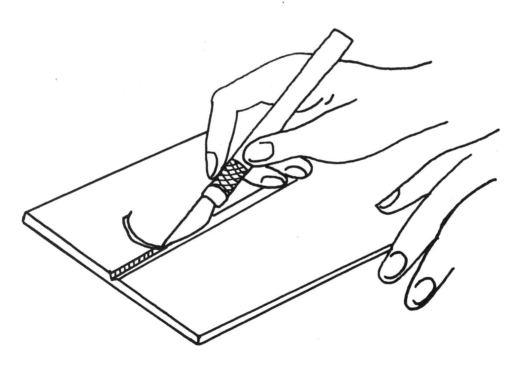

Cutting a crease with a craft knife.

34

then the other while holding the knife at a forty-five degree angle to produce a V-shaped notch. The notch should be less than one-half the thickness of the leather at its deepest part. After a groove is cut, even the heaviest leathers will fold easily. Note that this notch is always cut on the inside of the leather. For lighter leathers, merely fold the leather on the desired crease line without notching. If the skin resists folding, tap it lightly with a mallet.

Now take the folded leather and spread a thin coat of cement evenly across the inner surface. Spread another thin coat of cement on the lining piece. Let the cement dry for a few minutes before joining pieces. Then place the lining on one half of the leather right up to the crease. Smooth the lining and then refold the leather so that it is in the same shape as it will be when the project is completed. Then press the lining around the fold and turn the leather over. Smooth the remainder of the lining into place. Follow this process carefully as a lining that is glued to a folding part when flat will wrinkle. Cut away any excess lining after the cement has dried.

When attaching a smooth lining to a smooth leather, as when gluing two pieces of suede, it's advisable to use the two-coat method of cementing. This is done as with the folded lining; spread the cement on both pieces, allow them to dry a bit and then press them together while the glue is still tacky.

Linings for leather clothing are discussed in Chapter Six, along with sewing.

USING READY MADE PATTERNS:

Patterns are available from any of the major pattern companies and can be used to make all sorts of clothing and accessories such as pocketbooks, hats, gloves, etc. Many stores specializing in leathercraft supplies stock patterns designed specifically for leathercrafted clothes, others can be adapted.

To select a pattern, look through the catalogues and keep in mind that the simplest designs are often the best. Try to avoid styles with tucks, gathering or excessive detail as these are difficult to achieve well using leather. Make certain that the pattern is not intended for lightweight or stretch fabrics. Look for "easy to sew" designed patterns as they can be quite good to work with using leather.

For your first article of clothing, consult Chapter Ten of this book and start with something basic, like a vest, poncho, cape or skirt. These will usually have three or four main parts and not too many seams. The result can be an attractive wearable garment you'll be proud of.

Pick a pattern and take it with you when shopping for leather. This way you can be sure that you'll get the proper amount. You can always use leftover pieces to good advantage, but if you buy too little leather and then run out of it before finishing the garment. it will be difficult to match. Each dye lot varies a little even when it's supposed to be the same color, so try to buy enough the first time around. Here's a method to help you calculate your needs: The yardage for fabric will be printed on the envelope of the pattern and has to be converted to square feet for buying leather—that's how it's sold.

If the yardage listed is for thirty-six inch wide fabric, simply multiply this amount by nine and add on twenty per cent of the total. For example, two yards of thirty-six inch wide fabric is converted to leather square footage as follows; Two yards multiplied by nine equals eighteen. Twenty per cent of eighteen equals 3.60; 3.60 plus 18 equal 21.60 square feet of leather.

When the yardage listed for fabric is for fifty-four inch wide material, multiply by thirteen instead of nine. For example: Two yards of fifty-four inch fabric is converted as follows; $2 \times 13 = 26$, 20% of $26 = 5.20$, $26 + 5.20 = 31.20$ square feet of leather. The use of these two formulas will cover most situations in buying leather according to fabric yardage. If you're working with large skins, substitute fifteen per cent for the twenty per cent when calculating needs.

To cut out the pattern, lay it out on the leather. The largest sections should always follow the natural grain of the leather. This grain runs the length of the skin from the neck to the back. This is why the large sections should be laid lengthwise, it avoids stretching as with a crosswise grain and allows the garment to drape, or hang, better and more naturally when assembled. Small parts can be laid crosswise if desired or for the sake of economy of usage. Shift the pieces around and try them several ways on the skins to allow for the best use of the leather. Save any excess material, it always comes in handy and is too valuable to just discard. Good placement is economical, but be sure to avoid any visible blemishes that will mar the finished garment.

When a pattern calls for doubled fabric for cutting you'll have to do it in two stages as leather should never be cut when folded. Instead, cut out one half and turn the pattern piece over to cut the other half of the skin. Or, you can make a duplicate of the pattern piece out of wrapping paper. Use a tape or heavy weight to hold the pattern in place while you cut. Don't use pins unless you stick them into a seam allowance—pinholes won't disappear into leather the way they do with fabric. Cut the leather with sharp scissors or shears as you would any other pattern and remember to cut out the diamonds along the pattern edges as they are invaluable when putting the garment together.

One last hint on patterns: To assure correct size and fit of a garment before cutting the leather, it's a good idea to make a model of the article if you have any cause for doubts. Cut out the pattern from muslin or an old bed sheet and baste it lightly to try it on. Once you're satisfied with the fit of the model, you can cut and sew your leather with confidence. Keep in mind that leather clothing can't be easily let out as the stitches make permanent holes that can't be erased. Choose your pattern, follow these instructions and apply your own common sense as you proceed. The reward is a finished garment that will fit well and last for years.

CHAPTER FIVE

Lace It Up

The process of lacing, or thonging, is perhaps the most attractive, and certainly the strongest, method of attaching leather seams. Laces lend themselves well to almost any article or style and are not limited to one method of stitching. There are several stitch patterns to choose from, each is different in appearance and application.

BUYING LACES:

Laces can be bought from leather supply stores either by the yard or on spools. They usually come in black, some browns, white and several natural tans. They are made of calfskin, goatskin or cowhide. The width and weight of laces vary and should be selected with regard to the size and type of leather in the article to be laced. Smaller or lightweight leather articles should be laced with thin lightweight laces and so on.

Suede laces are almost always made of split cowhide and are available in various widths. They are limited as to color selection.

Vinyl laces are made in all colors, but these are not recommended for leatherwork as they are obviously imitation and will detract from the natural beauty of leathers on which they are used.

Other lacing materials can be bought and used for different effect, contrast or novelty—venetian blind cord, for example—but leather works best on itself.

MAKING LACES AT HOME:

Due to the color limitations of ready-made laces, you may prefer to make lacing from the same leather being used for the project. This can be easily done with most leathers, but should be avoided on suedes other than those made of split cowhide. The garment suedes are usually too soft and stretchable for making good lacing material.

There are several quick methods of cutting laces. They should be cut from one-eighth to one-quarter inch in width as needed, according to the size and weight of the project.

To start with, take a large enough skin or remnant and cut out a circular or oval piece of the leather. Then, using a knife and cutting board, a leather scissors or draw gauge knife, cut into the edge of the circle or oval until the desired width of the lace needed is obtained. Now, with the knife or scissors held parallel to the outer edge of the circle or oval piece of leather, start to cut a strip. Continue to cut, turning the leather with your free hand until the whole piece is used up. The spiral form will straighten out as it's used and you'll have one long lace.

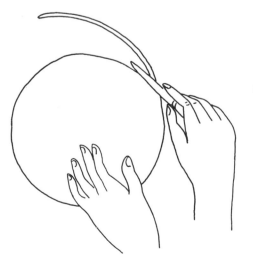

Cutting laces with a knife.

To make lacing from an odd-shaped piece of leather, slice into the edge as in the first method and continue to cut around the edge until you use up the piece or have the amount of lace you need.

To cut laces from a remnant or skin with a straight edge, place the leather on a cutting board work surface and use a metal ruler as a guide for your knife. A draw gauge knife can also be used to cut heavier weight laces on a straight edge.

A paper cutter, if available, can be used to cut laces from light or medium-weight leathers. Make certain the leather lies flat on the cutting table or it will bunch under the blade and result in an irregular cut.

Whichever method you use to make laces, go slowly and carefully to make sure of an even cut. Uneven laces are likely to stretch or break at thin spots and will be hard to work with. For the most part, when very thin laces are needed it may be best to buy them ready-made at first, as cutting them will be difficult.

MARKING SEAMS FOR LACING HOLES:

Marking the holes for laces is an important step which should not be overlooked. A few extra minutes spent before actually making the holes will insure even, attractive results.

Tools needed are:

Metal square, ruler or stitch gauge
Ballpoint pen or pencil

It's only necessary to mark one side of the seam. The marks can then be made on the other side through the holes on the first marked side after they have been punched. It is easiest to work by marking the corners first. The hole marks should be made in the center of the corner, about one-eighth to one-quarter inch in from the edge, depending on the size and weight of the leather being used. After the corner holes have been marked, use a pen and ruler and mark the places for the rest of the holes to correspond with the corner marks so that they are equal in distance from the edge of the leather. Whenever possible, try to make the space between each hole the same size as the space from the holes to the edge of the leather, so if the distance to the edge is one-eighth inch, the distance from one hole to the next should be one-eighth inch and so forth.

If you intend to use a stitch gauge, first mark a corner as explained and then select the wheel with a stitch space size that best matches the distance from the corner mark to the edge of the leather. Put the wheel on the leather and make sure that one of the points of the wheel is resting on the corner mark. Then, using a ruler's edge as a guide, push the stitch gauge firmly forward for even marking.

Note: If a thonging chisel is to be used on light to medium-weight leathers, only the corner holes have to be marked as a guide prior to punching.

Using a stitch gauge.

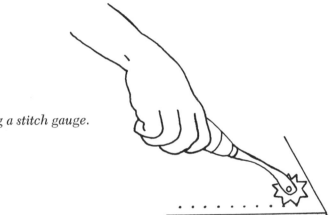

PUNCHING HOLES FOR LACING:

Tools needed are:

    Craft knife or scissors
    Rotary hole punch or drive punch and
    mallet or thonging chisels
    Rubber cement

If thonging chisels are to be used, it's best to have the single and three, or four, prong chisels. These are used with a mallet and cutting board.

Put the leather flat on the cutting board and hold the single prong chisel straight up and down with its point resting on the mark indicating the corner hole position. Strike the top of the chisel squarely with the mallet hard enough to cleanly pierce the leather.

After the corner holes have been pierced, use them as a guide for the three or four prong chisel. Place either one along the edge of the leather, leaving the desired space between the edge and the holes to be made, and strike it firmly with the mallet.

When the first set of holes has been made, use the last hole in the line as a guide; put the end prong of the chisel into it to make sure that the next set of holes is evenly spaced, and so on.

To punch holes with a rotary head punch, select the correct size tube for the laces by first making a few sample punches on a piece of scrap leather as being used in the project. Test the size by putting a lace through the sample holes. The lace should go through easily but should not have space around it once it is through the hole. You'll want the laces to fit snugly when you piece the article together. When you're satisfied as to the correct size of the holes on the scrap, go to work on your project holding the rotary puncher as you would a set of pliers.

A drive punch can be used in the same way, except the holes are made by holding the punch straight up and down, as with the pronged chisels, and striking the punch with a mallet or hammer.

When the holes are finished on the side of the already marked leather, lay the punched piece on the other side of the same seam and mark through the holes with a pen or pencil. This will insure that the seams will be even and the holes perfectly matched for even lacing. Then, punch the newly marked places using the same method as for the first half.

If very heavy leather is to be laced, hold the seams together and study their combined thickness. If the seam appears too thick or ungainly, you should skive, or thin, the inside (flesh side) of the leather as follows. Use any leather or skiving knife and cut about one-half the thickness from the flesh side of the leather. Hold the knife flat against the leather on a slight angle. The cutting should taper so that the leather is thinnest at the edge.

Do this to both of the pieces that will form the seam. Be careful not to thin too much or the holes may tear when laced.

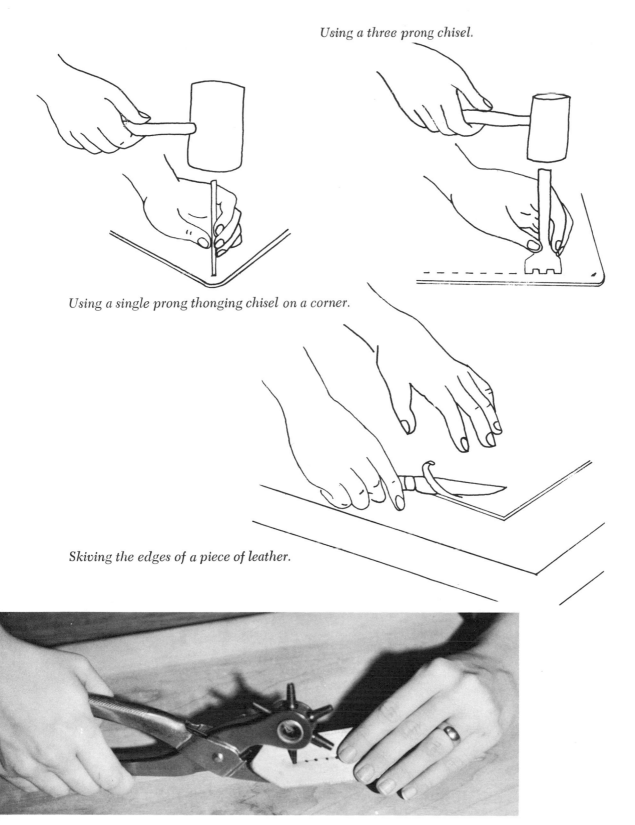

Using a three prong chisel.

Using a single prong thonging chisel on a corner.

Skiving the edges of a piece of leather.

Using a rotary punch.

As a last step before lacing, it's best to slightly round off and cut each corner, as it's hard to lace around a pointed end.

LACING STITCHES:

Tools needed:

Lacing needles
Rubber cement
Laces
Mallet

For best results and ease of handling, the lace you use should be no longer than a yard and a half or so. If the lace is much longer than this, pulling it through the many holes will stretch and weaken it. When a new lace is needed to continue a seam, it can be spliced to the remainder of the previous lace as follows:

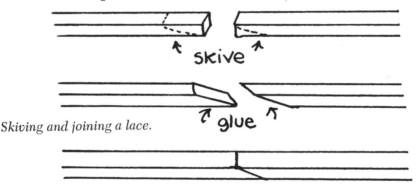

Skiving and joining a lace.

The joined lace should then be allowed to dry completely after the above three steps. Then continue lacing using one of the following methods:

THE RUNNING STITCH—as the name implies, this is a simple in and out stitch. The lace should first be skived a bit at one end and put in a lacing needle. The other end is skived and glued with a small amount of rubber cement to the inside of one seam as close to the holes as possible. The needle is then brought through the nearest hole and the running stitch continued by going in the next set of holes and out the following set.

44

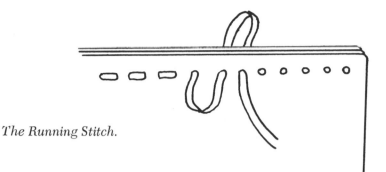

The Running Stitch.

When the end is reached, pull the lace between the two pieces that make up the seam and cut it off after leaving about one half inch excess which will then be glued as close to the holes as possible.

THE WHIPSTITCH—this is done by putting the lace in a needle and gluing the other end near the inside seam as with the running stitch. The needle is then brought from the back into the first hole, out the front, over the seam and into the back of the next hole.

In the above illustration, several stitches have been done this way and the glued piece between the two pieces of leather is outlined with a dotted line. When a corner is reached, it's best turned by making two stitches in the hole just before the corner and then two in the hole of the corner itself. This technique will cover the corner properly and add strength for longer wear.

An alternative way of doing this is to make three stitches in the corner hole alone, but getting the needle and lace through the hole the third time can be difficult. When you reach the end of the seam, insert the needle between the seams where the first stitch was made, cut the lace leaving about a half inch excess and cement it into place near the already glued beginning piece of lace.

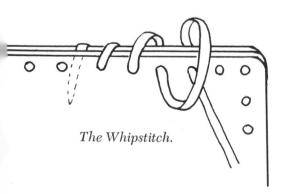

The Whipstitch.

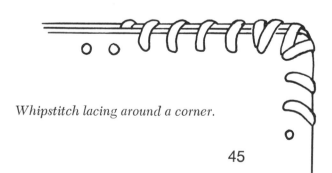

Whipstitch lacing around a corner.

45

THE FLORENTINE LACE—this type is done with a softer, wider lace that covers the edges of the seam while doing a regular whipstitch. It is the width and texture of the lace itself that gives it a different look. It folds up as it goes into the holes and widens as it covers the edges of the seam. It is done in the same way as the whipstitch.

Since the Florentine Lace is softer, it can be done on corners by simply going into the corner hole three times with no difficulty.

If you prefer, the hole near the corner can be laced twice and the corner hole twice as with the whipstitch. Both stitches are ended in the same way, leave half an inch excess and glue.

THE BUTTONHOLE STITCH—is a more complicated lacing method that forms its own edge to completely cover the pieces of leather where they are joined. It's started by lacing a needle, bringing it through the first hole and leaving a three inch piece of lace sticking up. The laced needle is then brought from the back and the lace is wrapped once around the three inch piece:

The needle is then put into the second hole and through the stitch made just above the second hole:

Then it is tightened:

Florentine lacing.

Florentine lacing around a corner.

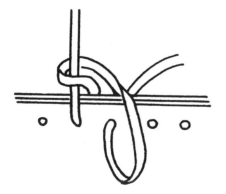

Starting the buttonhole stitch.

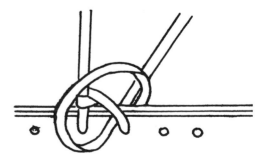

Second step in the buttonhole stitch.

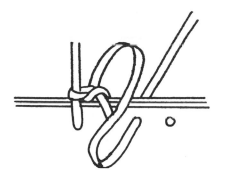

Tightening the buttonhole stitch.

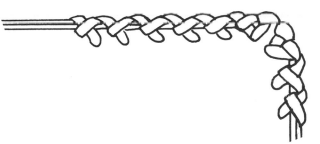

Lacing a corner with the buttonhole stitch.

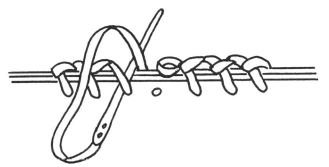

First stitch undone leaving a loop.

Ending the buttonhole stitch.

The rest of the article is laced the same way. In corners, it is again best to lace the hole that's just before the corner two times and then lace the corner hole twice. This stitch can also be laced three times into the corner hole if desired. In either case, be sure that the stitches are spread evenly around the corner:

To finish the buttonhole stitch at the end of the seam, lace it up to the first stitch and then carefully undo the first stitch leaving a loop:

The piece that is left should then be pulled through at the back in between the two pieces of leather that form the seam and cut off leaving one half inch for gluing close to the other stitches. The last stitch is then completed by going through the loop left by the first stitch and into the first hole:

The remaining lace is then pulled between the two pieces of leather and cut off to one half inch and glued right next to the other glued end of the lace. If you intend to use the buttonhole stitch on a seam that does not meet at the end, the first and last stitches should be done in a simple whipstitch.

THE DOUBLE CROSSTITCH—This is a very attractive lacing technique that uses two laces at the same time. Start by gluing the two lace ends right near the inside of the holes and put the other ends into two lacing needles. If you prefer, you can use one long lace with needles at both ends. Draw the lace through the first hole and leave half the length on each side of the leather.

The stitch is done by putting the needles through the same hole, either both at once or one at a time. Then they are crossed over the edge of the leather and inserted into the next hole:

This makes a very sturdy seam that can also be used for leather pieces that are being joined side by side or while flat:

A quicker cross stitch can be made by going into the next hole so that the stitches look the same from top and bottom, like a series of X's with a space between each one.

When you are finished lacing, lightly pound the completed seams with a mallet to flatten them.

If you intend to use a hammer in place of a mallet, place the article between sheets of paper or tissue before pounding. This will protect the leather from being scarred or dented by the metal head of the hammer. Light pounding gives the laced edges an even smooth appearance that will enhance the look of the entire project.

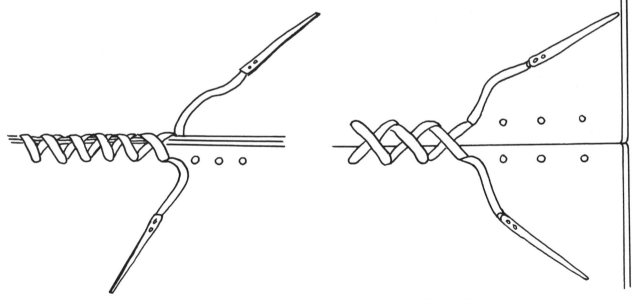

Double cross-stitch.   *Top view of the double cross-stitch on a flat seam.*

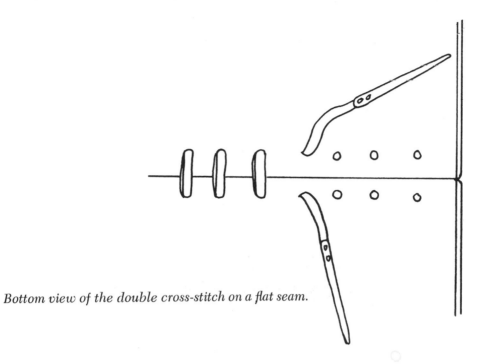

Bottom view of the double cross-stitch on a flat seam.

Flattening a laced seam with a mallet.

CHAPTER SIX

Sewing Leather Better

The sewing of leather is an attractive alternative to lacing often used for reasons of design, construction, appearance or personal preference. It can be done equally well by hand stitching or sewing machine and is of particular interest for the crafting of fine leather garments.

SEWING BY HAND:

Leather articles can be effectively hand sewn by using the right tools and the following techniques.

Tools needed:

Craft knife
Scissors
Shoemaker's awl
Stitch gauge or ruler
Two leather needles
Ball point pen or soft lead pencil
Waxed cotton thread or buttonhole twist
Silk thread
Pliers

PREPARING THE EDGES FOR SEWING:

To prepare the edges of leather for sewing, the weight and thickness of the hide should first be considered. If a heavier weight skin is being sewn, the inner edges to be joined should be carefully thinned, or skived. This will make the resulting seams less bulky. Skive with a craft knife, making certain that you cut away less than half the thickness of the leather on the flesh side of the hide along the seam edges.

The heavy leathers can further be prepared for sewing by hand by making a slight indentation or track for the stitches to lie in. This is done with a tool called an edge creaser. A smooth pointed object can achieve the same effect.

The edge creaser is simply pulled down along the edge of the grain side of the leather where the seam will be and results in an indentation.

Edge creasing tools are made in several sizes for various depths of seam placement. If a creaser is not available, use something like the tip of a knitting needle and a ruler to make an indentation along the desired line. There are also plastic or bone creasers available that should be used with a ruler, but in general you can make a substitution if necessary. Once skived and creased, the heavy leathers can then be handled just like light and medium weights for the rest of the sewing procedure.

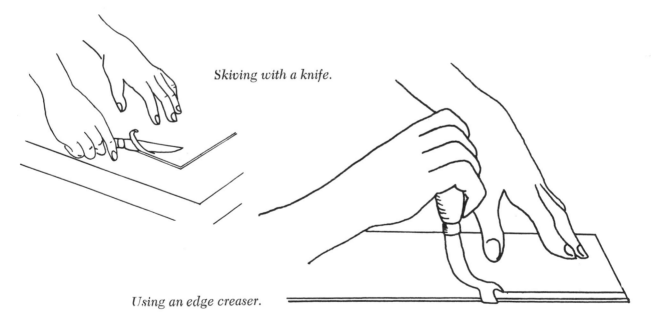

Skiving with a knife.

Using an edge creaser.

To mark the seams for stitch holes, use a stitch gauge. Most gauges have different size wheels for various weight leathers as well as distance between stitches. The lighter the leather, the smaller the spaces between the stitches should be; they can also be placed closer to the edge, but a border of one-eighth to one-quarter inch is recommended. The distance between stitches is mainly a matter of personal preference. The stitch gauge will provide a basis for choice, with the medium size being the most often selected.

In marking the seam, the gauge is drawn along in the indentation left by the creaser or at a chosen distance from the edge if no crease has been made; the small dots left by the gauge indicate where the stitches should be placed. When following a straight line where there is no crease, use a ruler to guide the stitch gauge. If desired, you can substitute a ruler and ball point pen in place of the stitch gauge to mark dots evenly for stitch placement. Remember, the stitches should be marked on one of the pieces that will make up the seam. Then, rubber cement the pieces together with the marked piece on top. The cement is applied only on the flesh, or inner, side of the seam as close to the edge as possible. The glued seam, when dry, is then pierced with a shoemaker's awl or icepick wherever you've previously made a dot with the stitch gauge or ball point pen. Be sure you penetrate both halves of the glued seam. The best way to do this is to place the leather on a cutting surface and push the awl down through the seam to the board below:

Heavy leathers can be held in a vise during this step in sewing; leave just the seam edge protruding from the jaws of the vise and pierce it with the awl.

If you prefer not to glue the seams together, or find yourself out of rubber cement, there is an alternative method of hole piercing. Again, only one half (or piece) of the seam is marked. Then pierce holes into the marked piece. Now lay the pierced seam half directly on the unmarked piece and use your pen or pencil to mark a corresponding line of dots where the holes should be made so the halves will match for sewing after both have been pierced. Match the halves carefully to mark the second piece or you may find yourself with an uneven edge when the holes are lined up to form the seam.

52

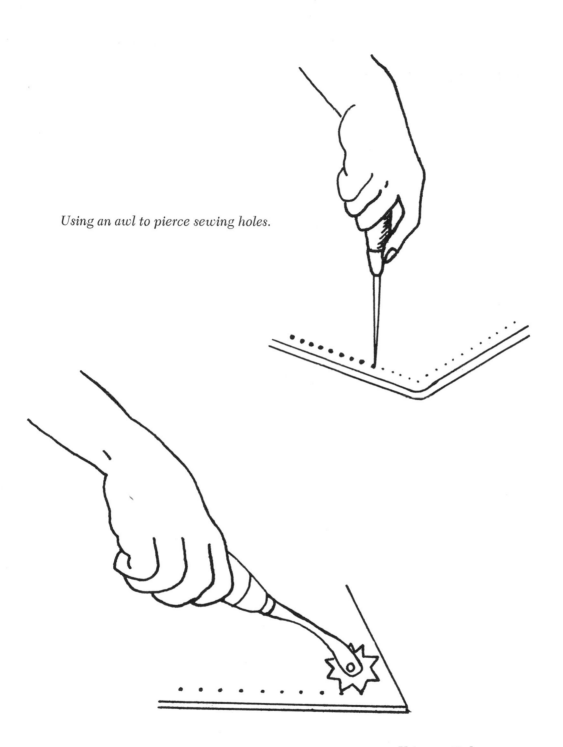

Using an awl to pierce sewing holes.

Using a stitch gauge.

STITCHES FOR HAND SEWING:

The Running Stitch is the most basic of all the sewing stitches. Glue one-half inch of your thread along the first few holes on the inside of the seam. Thread the free end into the needle and simply sew in one hole and out the next:

At the end of the seam, pull the thread between the two pieces of joined leather, cut the thread—leaving a half inch excess—and glue the excess in place as close to the stitches as possible, just as you did with the beginning half inch.

The Overcast Stitch is a stronger method of attaching visible seams. First glue a half inch piece of thread along the inside of the seam, thread your needle and bring it through the first hole. Continue sewing by passing the needle over the seam and going into the back of the next hole:

End the seam by bringing the thread between the two pieces of leather, cutting off after leaving a half inch excess and gluing the excess into place along the seam.

The Back Stitch is a good sturdy stitch for invisible seam making. Start by gluing and threading, as in the running and overcast stitches. Bring the needle out through the first hole to the back of the seam. Go into the back of the second hole, out the front and then into the front of the first hole again. Come out the back of the first hole and put the needle into the back of the third hole, out the front and then into the front of the second hole. Come out the back of the second hole and pass the needle through the back of the fourth hole, out the front and then into the front of the third hole. Come out the back of the third hole and into the back of the fifth hole and so on.

The seam is ended by pulling the thread between the two leather pieces that make up the seam, cut and glued in the same manner as the other stitch styles.

The Cobbler's Stitch should be used when an exceptionally strong binding is needed for either visible or invisible seams. This stitch is made using two needles and two threads. Or you can use one long thread with a needle at each end. For the two thread method, glue both thread ends to the inside of the seam. Thread both needles, one to a thread, and pass them through the first hole point to point. The stitch is made as if each needle is making a separate running stitch. The first needle goes into the second hole from the front and the other needle goes into the same hole from the back. The first needle then goes into the third hole from the back and the other needle goes into the same third hole from the front and so on:

The seam is ended by bringing both needles between the two pieces of leather, cutting and gluing.

For the one thread method: thread a needle at each end of a long piece of thread, draw it through the first hole leaving half the thread on each side and proceed as with the two thread method as explained and illustrated.

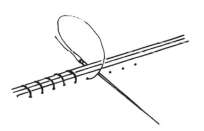

The overcast stitch.

The running stitch.

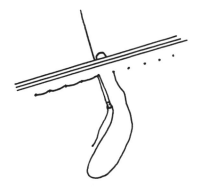

The back stitch.

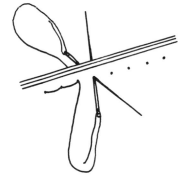

The cobbler's stitch.

THE SEWING AWL:

Hand sewing can also be done with the use of a leather sewing awl. There are several types available and each differs slightly in use. Manufacturer's instructions are included with each awl purchased and these should be read and followed. In general, sewing awls for leather are used on marked but unpierced edges. The awl makes its own holes as the needle is pushed through the leather to be joined:

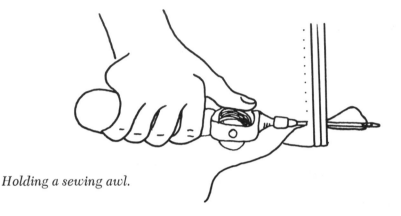

Holding a sewing awl.

SEWING BY MACHINE:

When making articles such as clothing, the soft, or light to medium weight leathers can be sewn on an ordinary home sewing machine by making a few small adaptations. The heavy leathers, however, should not be sewn on a home machine as the needles just aren't strong enough to pierce properly heavyweights when doubled, as they are in a seam. It is possible though to use a sewing machine without thread to pierce holes in heavy leather, one side at a time, and then sew the two pierced halves together by hand.

The first adaptation for sewing leather by machine is to replace your standard needle. Several special leather needles are available. They usually come in three sizes for light to medium weight leathers. Whenever possible, the first or smallest size needle should be used. The larger the needle the larger the hole, and that can be unattractive, since the thread size remains the same even though the hole may be bigger.

56

Start with the small one but if you find that you're having difficulty piercing the leather, switch immediately to the next larger size or the needle may break.

Next, to accommodate the extra thickness of leather as compared to cloth, the pressure of the pressure foot should be decreased somewhat. Although sewing machine booklets sometimes recommend increased pressure for heavy fabrics, this does not apply to leather. Fabric will compress as it goes under the pressure foot and then regain its shape somewhat. Leather will not.

If your machine does not have an adjustment to regulate the pressure foot, don't attempt to alter it as it will probably work just as it is and shouldn't be tampered with.

The stitch length lever or dial should be set at eight to ten for most leathers, but if you intend to sew a heavier leather, reduce it to six or seven. Don't try to use more stitches to the inch, even if it seems desirable. Too close stitches will tear the leather as do the perforations on the edge of a postage stamp.

Set the thread tension wheel fairly low, at about two or three. Try this setting out on a piece of scrap before beginning work on your actual seam. Check the results, if the tension is right for the job, the stitches will look the same on both sides. If you find that there are visible loops underneath the seam, then you should increase the tension. If the top thread looks tight, or the bobbin thread shows up in small loops, decrease the tension accordingly. The bobbin thread tension is adjusted automatically with the top, so change the top only and don't attempt to do anything on your own to the bobbin or bottom tension.

The thread used should be the new polyester core type or silk. The silk thread costs more than the polyester but it seems to work best and makes an attractive topstitched seam due to its own natural sheen. Cotton threads just aren't strong enough for machine sewing, even the mercerized type doesn't do the job well and isn't recommended. Nylon thread should be avoided as it's very likely to break due to the static electricity it builds up while sewing.

There's one thing left to check before sewing the actual garment or article. The feed dog on older machines is often made of metal and has little teeth to push the fabric along under the pressure foot. These metal teeth can scar leather, especially when the pressure foot cannot be regulated. So try it out on a piece of scrap leather. If there are little scratches on the underside of the leather tested, put a piece of thin paper over the feed dog and place the leather on top of the paper when sewing. The paper won't interfere with the sewing process and will protect the leather from the teeth. On many machines, the feed dog is made of hard rubber and won't harm the leather at all, so paper won't be necessary if this is the type you'll be working on.

Sewing leather clothing on a machine is somewhat different than sewing fabric, so here are a few pointers that can help you while working on, and finishing, leather garments.

Since leather will have permanent marks whenever stitches are made, a garment cannot be attractively let out once it is sewn. It is most efficient, and time-saving in the long run, to make a muslin or old sheet version of the garment being made, especially if the pattern is an unfamiliar one, as detailed in Chapter Four under the heading, "Using Ready Made Patterns". If you intend to use a pattern you've worked with before, this step can be eliminated, but you'll find that it's worth while to take the time to do it.

It's best not to try to sew leather too quickly—take your time. Run the machine at a moderate speed and proceed carefully for the most satisfying results. Even if you're an experienced machine operator and have already made your own clothes, don't rush when using leather.

After sewing, the seams of leather garments should be spread flat on the inside. The seam allowance is then flattened by light pounding with a mallet, glued into place on each side with a small amount of rubber cement and pounding lightly once more.

Flattening a seam with a mallet.

If you're using seam tape, hold it in place with a clip or pin before sewing. Be sure that the pin used pierces the seam allowance only. The taped seams should be flattened with a mallet, but gluing is optional.

There are three methods of ending a seam. Try each on a leather scrap and pick the one that suits you and the project best.

The first method is to leave two inches of extra thread at the end of the seam and tie these two pieces with several knots by hand.

The second way is to leave two inches of thread at the end of the seam, pull the bobbin thread until the top thread makes a small loop on the bobbin side, then pull this loop through with a pin and tie the two threads on the bobbin side of the seam by hand. It should be noted here that trying to end a seam by getting the needle to go back into the same holes with the machine in reverse is difficult.

The third method is to sew to the end of the seam, turn the work around and carefully sew five or six stitches into the same holes as the end stitches. Now cut the thread close to the leather on the top side of the seam and pull lightly on the bobbin thread to bring the small end piece through to the under side. Then cut the bobbin thread close to the leather.

When sewing a curved seam, proceed slowly to avoid going off the seam at an angle. Once the seam is made, take scissors and cut little V's in the top half of the seam allowances to assure smooth flat seams.

After the seams have been notched, flatten them with a mallet and cement.

To make good corner seams, round the points of the corner with scissors and follow the slightly rounded path while sewing. Pointed corners are difficult to turn and will result in a weak spot if sewn on a very sharp angle.

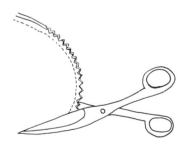

Cutting V's in a curved seam.

An attractive way to finish seams on leather clothing is to use single or double top stitching. In single top stitching, take both edges of the seam allowance and cement and flatten them both to one side. Then sew over both allowances close to the seam,

Single top stitching is best done on lighter weight leathers.

Double top stitching can be used on any leather that is sewable by machine. It's done on seams that are glued and flattened on both sides, as all seams are. The seam is then stitched on each side as near to the seam as desired. Be sure to include the seam allowance in the stitching.

Another quick version of top stitching is the lapped seam. Fold the seam allowance of one side of the seam before sewing. Glue it in place and pound lightly. Using a very small amount of cement, glue the folded half to the seam allowance of the other half of the seam. Let it dry. Then top stitch as near or far from the fold as you like, being sure to sew in all of the folded seam allowance—as this is the only stitching that will be done in this type of seam.

Darts should be cut with scissors after sewing and opened. Flatten, glue and flatten like other seams to avoid bulkiness.

Hems are made by simply glueing the hem into place with rubber cement. This may sound strange to an experienced fabric dressmaker, but it's the most efficient method, unless top stitching is desired as a part of the garment's design. When glueing a hem, spread the rubber cement on about an inch of the hemline and press it into place. If there is too much leather to glue easily, as in an A-line skirt, cut narrow V's into the leather wherever it puckers and then glue.

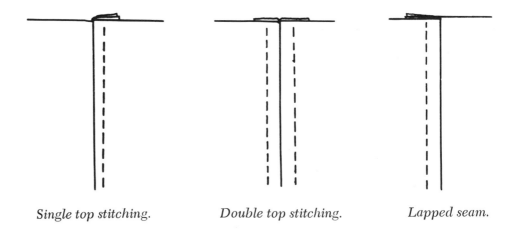

Single top stitching.   *Double top stitching.*   *Lapped seam.*

a) *Marked slot for buttonhole with two pieces of folded leather.*

b) *Top view of stitched buttonhole.*

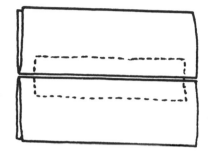

c) *Bottom view of stitched buttonhole.*

Buttonholes can be made as usual on a machine or by hand. They should be reinforced with a piece of matching scrap leather before sewing. Another way to do them is to cut a small rectangle the length of the button into the leather. Then glue two folded pieces of matching leather of slightly longer length to the inside and bottom of the rectangle and top stitch into place as illustrated.

The easiest way to do buttonholes is to select a pattern where loops or frog-type closings can be used. Another simple but attractively styled way is to use snaps in place of buttons and holes—as described and illustrated in Chapter Seven.

Zippers should be loosely glued into place with rubber cement to ease sewing. Then proceed as with any other zipper. A good idea is to use the new invisible zippers which are much easier to put in than the regular zippers and are more attractive when finished.

Many of the newest styles in leather clothing, particularly when done in reversible split suede, buckskin or cowhide, are not lined at

61

all. Although this is a break with tradition, these garments don't really need to be lined. The sueded cowhides don't stretch and will hold up well even without lining. If a lining is desired, it's best to make it as a separate unit and put it into the garment by sewing seam tape along the edges of the leather by machine and then sewing the lining in by hand. You can use any good lining material that does not generate static electricity. Taffeta and similar materials are durable and quite good. Pick an attractive color to either blend or contrast with the leather being used.

When the garment is finished, it can be pressed if necessary. Use a warm iron on the wrong side of the article making sure that you put a heavy paper or pressing cloth between the leather and the iron. Try the temperature setting of the iron on an extra piece of leather before pressing the garment and be sure that you're not striking while the iron is too hot.

CHAPTER SEVEN

Fastening and Decorating

Many of the fastenings seen on leather articles are functional as well as attractive. They're intended as a working part of the finished product and should be chosen and attached carefully to suit their proper purpose and best use.

SNAPS:

You'll find that snaps are among the most popular and versatile of the leather fastening devices. They're available in several sizes, weights and colors. Each size has a specific tool for setting it into leather, but the medium weight snaps can usually be set with one adaptable tool, as illustrated in this and Chapter Three, that's easy to work with as well as practical.

When buying snaps, check with the craft store as to which tool can be used with your selection, just to make certain. Whichever kind of snap you choose, the methods for secure setting remain the same.

Garment weight snaps are usually gold, silver, brown or black metal. There are also more noticeable snaps of the type used on Western

Snap parts: a) post b) spring c) eyelet d) cap

style clothing; these often have simulated pearl tops in white, blue, brown, or grey.

Snaps come in four pieces—two for the top half and two for the bottom. These parts are called the post, spring, eyelet and cap:

SETTING SNAPS:

For setting snaps that stay put, take a pencil or ball point pen and begin by marking a dot on the leather wherever you intend to place a snap. Then punch a hole of a size just large enough to accommodate the snap pieces snugly. Be certain not to make the hole too big for the snap as it may later work loose and the leather will tear. Check the hole size

Materials needed for snap setting.

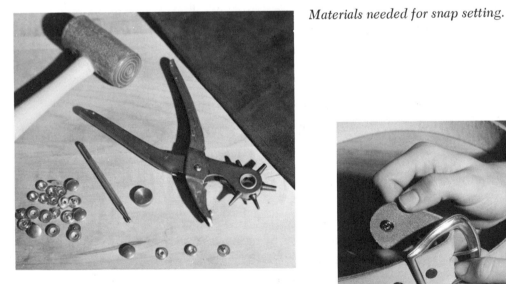

64

Using two snaps to set a buckle.

of your punch and snap on a piece of scrap leather before actually punching holes in your project.

Once you know the proper hole size, you can proceed as follows according to the tool you choose to use. To operate the rotary head punch, select the size from the choice on the rotary head. Make the hole where previously marked on the leather by holding the rotary head punch like a plier and positioning the punch head in place over the mark. Squeeze the handles together firmly until the hole is made. If you have difficulty reaching the area with the hand-held rotary punch, and no drive punch is available, you can try this adaptation; rotate the head until the correct size tube is exactly opposite its usual punching position. Turn the punch upside down with the tube held against the leather on the marked spot. Strike the punch over the bottom of the inverted punch head with a mallet to make the hole.

To use a drive punch, first lay the leather out on a cutting board work surface, place the punch over the marked spot on the leather and hit the punch top firmly with a mallet.

After all the holes have been made, the snap can be set as follows: Notice that the snap-setting tools have three parts; the anvil, with two sides, and two rods, possibly with small hammer-like handles. Each side of the anvil is fitted to one of the rods. The shapes of the anvil and two rods are so designed as to accommodate the top and bottom parts of the snap and are visibly different. It will be readily apparent which parts are used together.

To set the top half of the snap—the cap and eyelet—fit the eyelet on the correct half of the anvil. Place the hole in the leather onto the eyelet and put the cap on top. Now, with the concave rod on the cap, strike the rod with a mallet.

The result is that the top half of the snap will now be in place. For the bottom half setting; put the post on the other side of the anvil. Fit the hole in the leather onto the post and put the spring half on top of the now protruding post. Place the second rod on the spring and strike it with the mallet.

The second half of the snap is now in place. This method applies mainly to garment or medium weight snaps. The smaller glove snaps and larger heavy duty snaps are applied in the same general way and present no problem when the proper size tool is used.

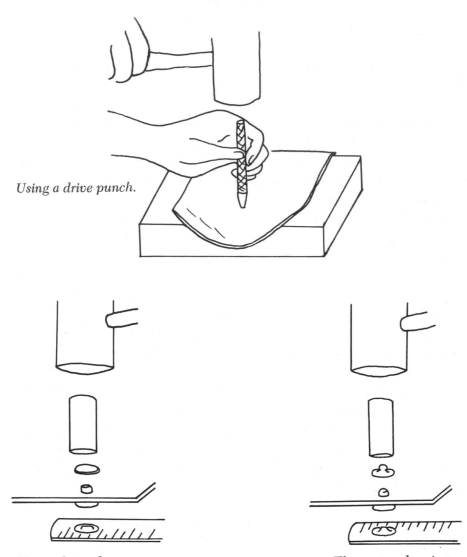

Using a drive punch.

The eyelet and cap.   *The post and spring.*

EYELETS AND GROMMETS:

Eyelets and grommets are used to reinforce holes in leather belts and other articles. Eyelets are available in several sizes and colors such as, gold or silver tone, brown, white, black and navy. They are attached to the leather after a hole has been punched. Grommets are usually made in the gold tone color, but other shades may in time become available.

Although grommets and eyelets are attached using their own special tool, more and more different type tools are being made that adapt for

66

use in several kinds of operation. For example, there are hand grip eyelet setters that can be converted to use in setting snaps. So remember, although the tools described here are for specific purposes and usually the most efficient for those purposes, it is very possible to apply a few of these different attachments with one type tool. Consult the chapter on Tools of the Trade for money-saving substitution ideas and check with the supply store you buy in as to the exact specifications of each tool purchased, and avoid unnecessary duplication. In any case, the general principles and instructions remain the same whether you have a specific tool for each operation or are making do with an adaptable workhorse.

Eyelets are made so that the edges of one side splay outward upon attachment. Grommets come in two pieces that are then pressed together so that both sides of a set grommet look the same. To set either eyelet or grommet: mark and punch a hole of exactly the size as the tubular part of the eyelet or grommet. Don't make the hole too big or the eyelet or grommet won't properly serve its reinforcing function. When the hole has been made, set an eyelet by putting it through the hole with a hand-held rotary punch or drive punch. The rim of the eyelet remains on the top side of the hole and the tubular shaft extends through the hole and out the bottom side. If an eyelet spreader is to be used, place the point of the spreader onto the tube from the bottom side and strike the spreader with a mallet.

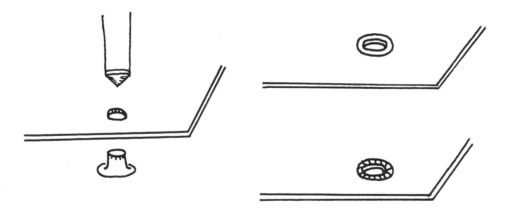

a) Setting an eyelet.   b) Top and bottom view of set eyelet.

Lining up a grommet to be set.

Hand-grip eyelet spreaders are pressed closed like pliers while clamped around the eyelet on top and bottom.

To set a grommet, put the tubular half in place on the bottom part of the grommet setter. Place the punched leather, outside down, so that the hole is over the grommet half. Put the top of the grommet on top of the hole in the leather and fit the pointed top part of the grommet setter into the grommet and strike with a mallet or hammer.

RIVETS:

Rivets are made of two pieces of metal, which when hammered together form a permanent closure. This type is called a rapid rivet. Like snaps, they come in a few sizes and colors, such as gold, silver, brown, black and white.

To set a rivet, mark and punch a hole of the same size as the rivet post into each of the pieces of leather you want to attach.

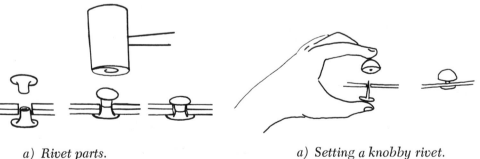

a) *Rivet parts.*
b) *Rivet being set using a mallet.*
c) *Set rivet.*

a) *Setting a knobby rivet.*
b) *Set knobby rivet.*

68

The bottom half of the rivet is a post that is placed below and through the two pieces of leather. The upper half is a cap-like piece that is put on top of the hole. The rivet is then struck with a mallet.

If you want to set a series of rivets, it's a good idea to first mark and punch all the holes necessary before setting any of the rivets. Another type rivet available consists of a one-piece unit with a split shank, or shaft. This is attached by placing it through the punched hole in the leather and then bending the two parts of the shank outwards using a mallet or hammer. These split rivets aren't very attractive and can cause discomfort if used on clothing, because of the edges of the split shank. Knobby rivets come with a domed top and sharp post with a flat bottom and are applied by simply pinching them into place on the leather. Neither the split nor the knobby rivets are as smooth inside as the rapid rivets are and shouldn't be used on areas that will come into contact with your skin.

CLEATS:

A useful variation of the split rivet is the cleat. Cleats are large and dome shaped and come mainly in gold and silver tones. They help to protect the bottoms of large handbags or suitcases and are invaluable for use on briefcases of all sizes. Cleats are attached by marking and making a hole; use a rotary or drive punch. Take the cleat and put the split prongs through the hole. Bend one prong to one side and one to the other leaving the ball end out to protect the leather from scuffing. Use a mallet or pliers to bend the prongs well.

a) Setting a cleat. b) Set cleat.

CLASPS:

Many pocketbooks and handbags are designed with a flap that can be closed with a clasp. Clasps are most often made of gold or silver tone metal. They come in four parts; the clasp itself, a plate which secures it to the leather, the slot the clasp button fits through and a plate to secure the clasp button.

The bottom, or clasp part, is fitted to the bag itself by selecting the correct spot on the leather article for it and marking the spot by pressing the four prongs on the bottom of the clasp to the spot. The result is four prong marks that indicate where to make four incisions with a shoemaker's awl, or a single prong thonging chisel and mallet. Once you've made the incisions, push the four prongs through them. Now place the plate over the protruding prongs and then bend the prongs flat against the plate. Cement a small patch of thin leather over the plate to cover it completely.

The slot part is attached by measuring the exact size of the opening and matching this rectangular shape to a place on the flap where

a) *Marking prong slits for a clasp.*
b) *Clasp prongs in leather with plate beneath.*
c) *Clasp set.*

a) *Marking slot for clasp slot.*
b) *Clasp slot in cut leather with plate beneath.*
c) *Slot set, top and bottom views.*

it will close comfortably over the clasp. This shape is then cut from the leather with a craft knife and the metal slot fitted into the cut hole and through the plate on the other side. Then bend the prongs of the slot down into place.

BUCKLES:

Most belts are closed by means of a buckle. There are numerous types of buckle to choose from, plain and fancy. Most of the various types are attached to a belt or strap in the same way. To start with, two inches should be left in the leather beyond the point where the buckle will be placed. At this two inch point, cut an oblong hole with a craft knife or by using the oblong hole puncher and a mallet.

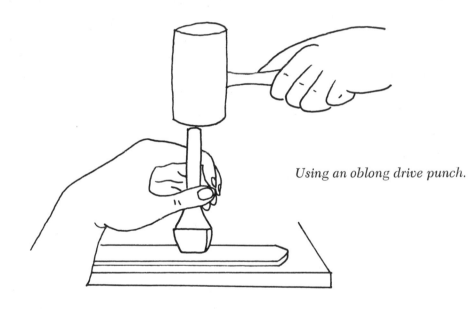

Using an oblong drive punch.

The hole you make is needed to accommodate the tongue of the buckle, which is slipped through the hole. The rounded part of the buckle remains above the leather. The remaining two inches of leather is then folded back to the body of the belt and sewn into place. If you prefer, two snaps can be placed at intervals along the two inch excess to allow for removal of the buckle.

71

Other devices are designed for use in leatherwork as purely ornamental attachments. These can all add beauty and individuality to an object by creating pattern and design accents of your choosing.

STUDS, SPOTS AND STARS:

Of the several metal ornaments made for leather, the most popular are the studs, or spots. They come in many shapes and sizes of different colors. The versatile dome or pointed dome shapes in gold and silver tone metal are a great favorite among leathercrafters and users. There are also star, heart and flower shapes made in various colors. Jeweled top spots in yellow, blue, green and red are available. New shapes and colors are being made and a browse through your supplier's catalogue will fire your decorating imagination. They're easy to attach and the results can sometimes be startling. Here's how it's done:

Studs are made with two to five prongs on a cap. The prongs can first be lightly pushed onto the leather in a selected spot or pattern. This will leave dots where the leather will be pierced. Take an awl or one prong thonging chisel and mallet pierce the leather at the marked places. Then, push the prongs of the stud through the holes made by the awl and bend them flat on the inside of the leather to hold them firmly in place.

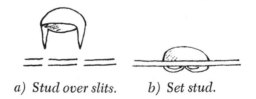

a) Stud over slits.   b) Set stud.

These spots, or studs, can be placed wherever they seem to best complement the article, either a hand-crafted or ready-made one. Use the design that interests you or just highlight or add accent by the use of just a few. For example; a belt could have a single, or double, row of domed studs placed around its edges. A pocketbook could have its flap or pocket outlined with flat head or star studs. A wide belt or vest pocket could be enhanced by a paisley or zig-zag design in studs of any shape or color. It's entirely up to you. These decorations and attachments are easy to work with and apply. You can place them in the

72

pattern of a projected design on the leather and see what it will look like before you mark or punch holes. That way you can change it around if the design doesn't suit you.

Another way to decorate is to use eyelets as design whether or not there's a need for reinforcement. They can also be used in ornamental whipstitch lacing; put one eyelet in each hole before lacing. The combination and designs are endless, and they're fun too.

Setting spots, or studs, with an awl.

APPLIQUES:

Appliques have recently become very popular and widespread in their use in leatherwork. They are shapes, cut from leather, suede or snakeskin which are glued or sewn into place. Their colors can be matched to the project or chosen for contrast.

Appliques that are sewn on seem to have a particular charm, although the glued ones are quite secure. They can be lightly glued for sewing, making them even easier to handle. To hand sew, follow the procedure of marking and piercing the leather to be sewn and use the back stitch as described in Chapter Six. For machine use, sew the appliques on before the project is assembled. An interesting variation is to lightly stuff the applique with cotton or lambswool, glue the edges in place and then sew. This gives the effect of a raised applique that looks particularly good when done in natural shapes like fruit, clouds, trees and flowers. Geometric and abstract shapes can be cut from scraps and sewn or pasted into place. A multi-colored bunch of findings, trimmed and arranged on an old leather belt is an excellent use of odd shapes and sizes put to use for decoration. You can even fashion a picture in leather and suede.

LACED APPLIQUES:

Laced appliques are cut out in the same way as the regular kind, but then a hole of the same shape but slightly larger is cut into the leather of the project. Stitching holes are then marked and punched around the edges of both the applique and the hole in the project and the applique is laced into place. Use the whipstitch or cross stitch. This type of decoration is most effective when done in basic, simple shapes— and it is easier to cut the design into the leather of the project when the shapes aren't too busy.

CUT OUTS:

You can make these by first cutting a design you've chosen into the leather of a project. Here, as with laced appliques, the basic shapes that are uncomplicated, like a star or even a butterfly, are the best and easiest to work with. After cutting, glue or sew a contrasting color to the wrong side of the leather. The color will be seen through the cut shape, almost like an applique in reverse. Some good backings to use for color or material contrast are thin leather, suede, snakeskin and even fabric in small prints or solids.

PATCHWORK:

Here's a way to use scrap pieces and odds and ends—or findings, as they are called—as the basic material of a project. First sew them all together with a sewing machine; the result is a patchwork hide you can use like a solid skin. Use leather, suede or both together—but for best results, just make sure that they're all similar in weight or thickness. Mix or match your colors, it's up to you and your supply of findings.

FRINGE:

The influence of American Indian and Western fashion has brought about a new appreciation of fringe on many leather articles and clothing. There are two ways of making fringes for your project. The first is to leave an allowance in the pattern itself according to the size fringe you want, then just cut the fringes into this allowance. Start by marking strips with a ruler and pen on the wrong side of the leather. Make the lines three-eighths to one-half inch apart. Then, cut the lines using a scissors or craft knife. If you're using a knife, guide the blade along the edge of a ruler for greater accuracy; on light leathers, scissors are easier to use.

The second way to make fringes is to cut the fringe separately from a strip of leather, leaving three-quarters of an inch at the top, and sewing the resulting fringe to the garment or article. This can be done in contrasting colors or anything that complements the article.

TASSELS:

Tassels are a traditional leather ornament and are so easy to make. Cut a strip of leather, between two and three inches wide, and four to six inches long. With a pen and ruler, mark up to three-quarters of the width of the strip in one-quarter to three-eighths inch strips. Be sure to make all your markings on the wrong side of the leather, the part that won't show. Now cut along these lines with a scissor or craft knife. Cut the last strip off completely. Glue this last strip to the inside of the long piece in the upper left hand corner. Spread glue along the rest of the uncut top border of the leather and roll it up. Use the strip in the upper corner as the center of the roll. This strip then sticks out of the completed tassel for easy attachment to the intended article.

BRAIDING LEATHER:

A lovely belt can be made simply by braiding leather. The strips can be of any desired length and width. If heavy leather is being used, cut the strips with a draw gauge knife. Set the width of the strip on the knife by checking the ruler that's built right into the tool. Then put the knife at the end of a straight-edged piece of leather and pull the knife slowly towards you. The blade will cut the correct width of leather strip as it goes.

You can also cut the strips with a craft knife and ruler or by using a scissors if the leather isn't too heavy. You then braid your three strips of leather in the same manner as any three strand braid. Even small children can have fun here while making something useful and attractive. For more complicated braids, such as those made with four or five strands, there is a basic rule you can follow. Lay the strips of leather flat and tape or otherwise hold all the ends on one side in place to ease handling.

The left outside strip is always the first one to move. It's crossed over the next strip and left there. Then the right outside strip is moved. When, as in the illustrated four braid strip, there is an even number of strips, the right side always goes under the strip next to it and is left there. Then the new right outside strip goes under the one next to it and so on. When there is an odd number of strips, as in the five strand braid, the first step is the same—left outside over the one next to it—and the right outside strip always goes over the strip next to it, under the next, over the next, until it is next to, but not crossing the last strip. The left, last, strip then crosses over the one next to it and braiding begins again from the right. In all cases, however, the left outside strip starts by crossing over the one next to it; the right outside strip always goes under the next strand in an even number and over the next strand in an odd number. Using this method, any number of strips can be braided to your liking. For a practice run, why not try braiding some pieces of yarn of different colors, see for yourself how each strip moves within the braid.

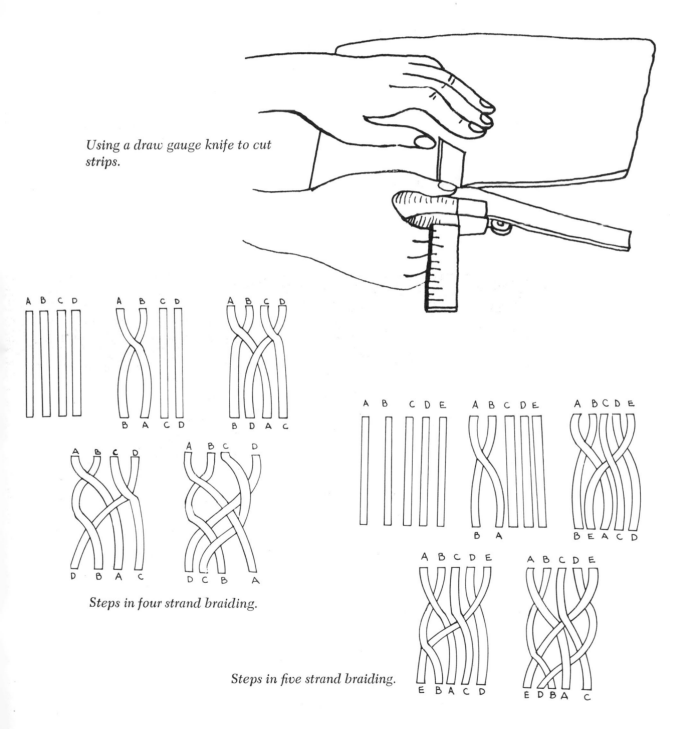

Using a draw gauge knife to cut strips.

Steps in four strand braiding.

Steps in five strand braiding.

EMBROIDERY:

Embroidery can be successfully done on softer leathers and suedes. Use an extra sharp needle. Anyone with a basic knowledge of embroidery stitches will be able to produce the same appealing effect of embroidered cloth on leather. Take a scrap piece of leather and try a few stitches until you get the feel of sewing leather in this manner. For those with sewing machines equipped with attachments to do embroidery stitches, these attachments can be used equally well on leather and suede. Just take the same steps you would as in regular machine sewing of leather. But whichever method you choose to attain appealing results, remember not to place your stitches near any points of stress or strain in the garment or article, the many needle holes made in the embroidering would weaken the leather at that point and the garment might tear when worn.

LARGE EYE BEADS:

Large eye beads, called crow beads, are made of glass or plastic and

Using large eye beads on leather fringe.

come in many colors. The glass beads have particularly good hues. Beads can be used in several ways to add accent or a touch of color to leather work. For instance, while lacing a suede article using the fairly wide lacing of the whipstitch, string a bead onto the lace every other stitch or so, it's an interesting effect. Beads can also be strung onto fringes; since they crimp the fringe a bit, they can't fall off. If a belt you make is to be tied with strips of leather instead of buckled, bead some of the strips.

SHELLS AND FEATHERS:

You may want to decorate your leather articles by the addition of seashells or feathers. A seashell has to have a hole drilled in it to allow for firm attachment onto your leather article. This is easier to do than it sounds, if you haven't a hand or electric drill, almost any sharp pointed tool will do as well: just hold the shell firmly on your work surface and gently bore a hole. You can now attach the shell by lacing or sewing through the hole. One large flat shell on a pocket book flap is one way of using shells on leatherwork, or just hang a scallop or other pretty shell on a leather loop and tie it around your neck, arm, waist or wherever.

Feathers are usually sold in millinery supply stores in ready-made rosettes and strips. These can then be sewn onto leather by hand. You can also get individual feathers to use in a design or grouping of your own.

RIBBONS, BRAID AND RICKRACK:

Patterned or plain ribbons, silk braid or rick rack can all be used easily, and with lovely results, on handbags, belts, hats, or just about any garment. They are most easily sewn on by machine using a contrasting or matching shade of thread. You can choose the particular ribbon, braid or rick rack according to the style and color of the object they'll be used on. First plan where the strips will be placed. They're usually best for borders and accents, but that's really up to you. Leather itself is attractive, so you don't have to worry too much about the addition of a little decoration.

CROCHET AND MACRAME:

Another idea for leathercrafters is to mix the media once in awhile. This interesting effect can be created by using crochet or macrame to link pieces of leather together to form vests, belts, pocketbooks, hats, capes and any other article it looks good with. This first requires a basic knowledge of crocheting or the knot-making of macrame. It's easily acquired. To attach the wool or cords is equally simple: holes are punched around the edges of the leather with a drive or rotary punch. The wool in crocheting is pulled through with a crochet hook and attached. Macrame cords are attached with the simplest knot. The wool or cord is then worked until it meets the other half of the seam which has been similarly attached. Once you know a little about crochet or macrame, the method becomes apparent.

INCISED LACES:

Incised laces are used in a decorative way on leather or suede of any thickness. The object is to create a design on the surface of the leather by lacing in and out through slits marked and cut into the leather. The easiest way to describe this lacing is to show its application on a leather belt. Take the strip of leather to be used for the belt and mark slits in the belt to accommodate the width of the lace to be used. Form a pattern or design of your choice. For a two inch wide belt, for example, five rows of slits could be marked and then made to accommodate five separate laces.

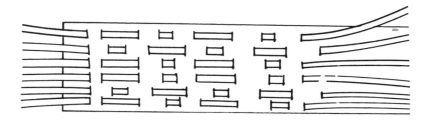

Incised lacing.

If you use a craft knife, remember to lay the belt flat to the work surface for easier cutting of the slits. You can leave six or more inches of lacing at each side of the belt and use the lacing to tie the belt closed, eliminating the need for a buckle. An attractive variation on this method is to use large eye beads and lip one on a lace. The beads will become permanently affixed to the belt since the lace will go into a slit after each bead is slipped into place.

Decorations are up to you, try almost anything, you'll be happily surprised with the results.

CHAPTER EIGHT

Tooling and Carving

There are many people who enjoy the art of tooling and carving leather. Tooled leather can be most attractive especially when done on smaller articles.

The skins must be moistened to correctly take the impressions later made with tools, so tooling and carving is best done only on vegetable tanned leathers; suede is not a good medium for this art. The properties of chrome or other chemically tanned leathers are such that moistening and tooling are very difficult, if not impossible.

Suitable carving leathers come in a few grades. Try working with a lesser grade at first, develop a feeling for the process and then when you're ready, go on to the better grades of leather. The difference between the grades is only that of the amount of scars or defects there are on a hide or skin, so it's often very simple to work around these defects or incorporate them into your design. For small articles in particular, it can mean a real savings on material.

Work done on lighter weight leathers is generally known as tooling, and stamping—if there is any. Work on heavier weights is called carving, and can be augmented with stamping. The tools for both are pretty much the same, except that the swivel knife described later is used only for carving. Tooling and carving is done on leather pieces of an article after the pieces have been cut to shape but before they are stitched or otherwise assembled.

The tools needed to start with are a rawhide maul or mallet of the sort used throughout the book for drive punches and other tools. It should be noted that a light-weight hammer isn't a good substitution for a rawhide mallet as it will drive the stamping tools too far into the leather surface and result in impressions that are too deep. Swivel knives are used for carving leather, they come with interchangeable blades for use on various weights of leather. Tracing and modelling tools are used to transfer and deepen the designs to be tooled onto the surface of the leather. They come with two ends, one smaller than the other, but both of identical shape. The basic modelling tool shown in the first illustration is for transfer of designs. The deerfoot modelling tool in the second illustration is for deepening outlines. The ball end modelling foot is used for embossing.

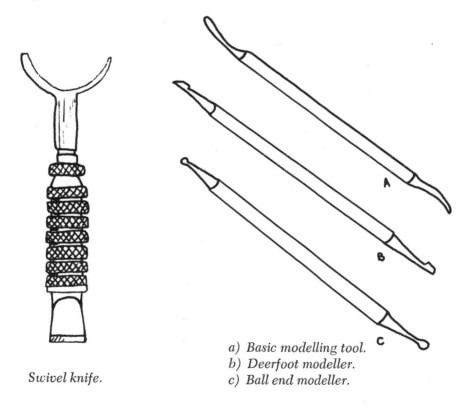

Swivel knife.

a) *Basic modelling tool.*
b) *Deerfoot modeller.*
c) *Ball end modeller.*

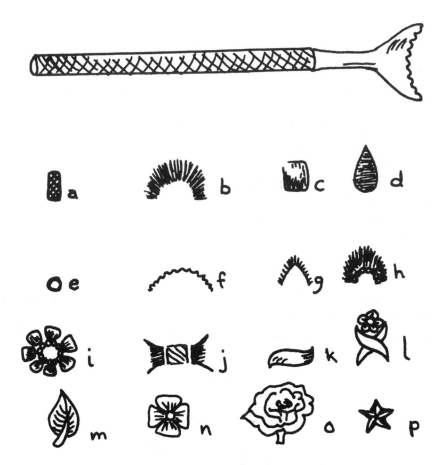

Typical stamping tool and impressions.

For beginning work, you'll find that one basic modelling tool will get you started nicely.

Stamping tools are available in numerous categories, shapes and sizes. The handle of the tool remains the same in any case. The tip is changed for each different impression. To begin with, you can select one stamping tool from each general category necessary for your design work and then add to your collection as your needs and interests require:

The tool illustrated above is called a veiner. Beneath the veiner are the impressions made by one from each of the categories of typical stamping tools:

A. GROUNDER—for background stamping

B. CAMOUFLAGE—for retouching and/or the addition of texture to a design

C. BEVELER—to produce a raised effect by depressing outlines

D. PEAR SHADER— for shading and contrast

E. SEEDER—used to make flower centers

F. VEINER—adds accents to leaves and other similar parts of the design

G. MULEFOOT—for retouching flowers

H. SUNBURST—figure work and texture tool

I. FLOWER CENTER—used in place of a seeder

J. BASKET WEAVE—border work

K. ROPE—for borders

L. BORDER STAMP

M. LEAF

N. FLOWER

O. ROSE

P. STAR

The list is a small sample of the various figure stamps available. There are also letters and numbers to monogram or design with.

TOOLING AND STAMPING LIGHTWEIGHT LEATHERS:

The design for tooling should first be copied on tracing paper from its source. There are many books that contain patterns explicitly devised for tooling. It's also easy, and more satisfying too, to adapt or originate your own pattern or design. The most important thing to consider is the balance between the design and the object to be worked on. Large or busy patterns seem to go best on larger projects. The traditional Western designs need not be the only ones considered either, an object of any type can be the inspiration for your tooling work. Although flowers and leaves remain the most popular ingredient of a tooled leather design, simple shapes, like animals, branches, fruit or abstract geometrics can be copied onto a project. Start with a paper replica of your intended design and object and see how the design will fit when finished. For your first project, choose some simple or basic design and work with it to get the feel of the tools on the leather.

To prepare lightweight leathers for tooling, they must first be moistened. Work on one piece of your intended project at a time. Put the leather on a hard smooth surface and moisten the flesh side with a dampened sponge; don't use a metal cup to hold the water, the metal may discolor the leather before you know it, use a glass bowl or dish. Now turn the dampened leather over and dampen the grain side. When the top and bottom sides are evenly moistened, both will be evenly darkened, but without blotchiness or light areas. Let the flesh side rest on the hard surface and allow the leather to dry until its surface begins to lighten. Once the surface is near its original color shade, it's ready for work. An easy way to test this is to moisten a scrap piece of the same leather along with the project leather itself. When you think the leather's ready, test the scrap for dampness by pressing it with a modeler. If the leather dents without any excess water seeping out of it, you can proceed with the project. But if water is visible in the depressed leather, wait awhile and then test it again.

The moistened leather, now dried to the correct dampness, should be left on the hard surface and the traced pattern placed on top of the area to be carved or tooled. Attach the pattern to the leather with clips or tape and leave one end free to raise and check on your tracing from time to time. Using the basic modelling tool, firmly and smoothly trace once over every line in your pattern. This will produce a clear but faint

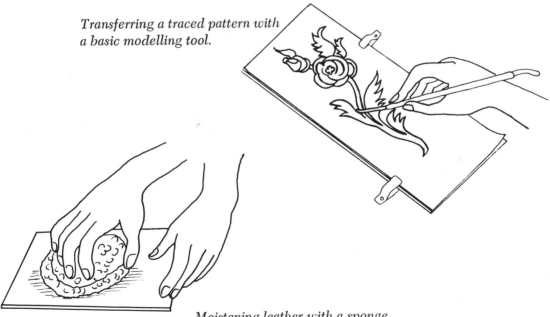

Transferring a traced pattern with a basic modelling tool.

Moistening leather with a sponge.

outline you can follow on the leather. If any of the lines are too faint, go over them after the paper tracing has been removed.

Remove the paper pattern from the leather once you are sure the entire design has been copied intact. Use the small end of the modeller to go over each line, deepening the impression on the leather's surface. If the depth of the outline is to be increased, to make the pattern stand out more clearly, turn the modeller over and use its broader side to further deepen the lines. This simple tooled pattern can be finished even at this stage in the method; it's called flat or outline tooling, as well as flat modelling.

The design can be further enriched, if desired, by the use of stamping tools. The stamp itself is held perpendicular to the leather and struck with a rawhide mallet. A good way to finish this type of pattern would be to select a grounder of any style and carefully stamp around the outlined pattern to create a textured background. To make a good background, the stamp should be placed right next to each impression as it is made, to fill in the empty space completely.

Another touch that can be attractive is the use of the border stamp to create a frame around the design.

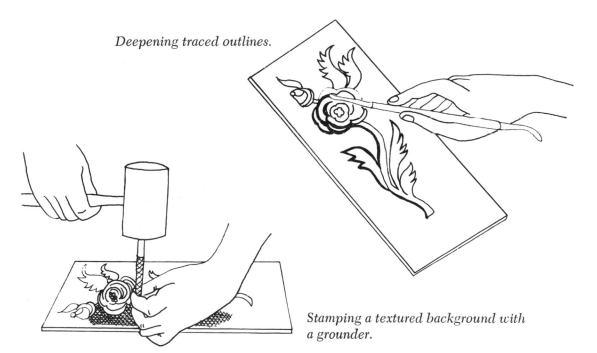

Deepening traced outlines.

Stamping a textured background with a grounder.

CARVING AND STAMPING HEAVYWEIGHT LEATHER:

Moistening heavy leather can often be done using the method described for lightweight skins. Some very heavy saddle or strap leathers, however, must first be washed with saddle soap, or hand soap—but not detergents —to loosen any dirt which may be lurking in the hide. After cleaning, remove all the soap, be thorough, and soak the leather briefly in a bowl of clear water. Remove the leather from the water and allow it to dry flat on a smooth surface until the hide lightens. Test a scrap piece for moisture by pressing with a modeller and looking for signs of water. The leather shouldn't show visible moisture or it will stretch while working it.

Transfer the design onto the damp leather with a modelling tool, the same way it is traced on lightweight leather. This design is now ready to be carved or cut into the surface with a swivel knife. This knife is used by placing your forefinger in the saddle on top of the knife. Hold the shaft with your thumb and other fingers on an angle away from your body and cut towards you for best control. The shaft, or barrel, of the knife swivels in the direction desired by a twist of your thumb and fingers. The aim is to cut a bit less than one half of the depth of the leather while making a smooth open cut throughout. It's a good idea to practice a while on moistened scrap leather before cutting your project. This practice can be important, as a cut wrongly done cannot be remade and shouldn't be done twice on the same line. Always hold

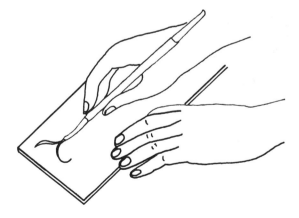

Holding a modelling tool.

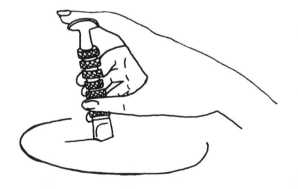

Holding a swivel knife.

the knife straight up and down while working and don't let it slip to the right or left, especially when making curved cuts. If the knife is held to the right or left, the fact will become readily apparent as it will cut a flap rather than a smooth open line.

Run a damp sponge over the traced lines in your project in case the leather has dried too much to be carved. Using the swivel knife, carve all the lines. If you reach another line while cutting, lift the knife and start again on the other side. Be certain you do this each time; two lines should never be cut over each other. Turn the leather as you work so that the knife is always pulled toward you. If there are straight lines to be cut, a plastic or wood ruler can be used; some metal rulers will stain dampened leather. If you have any difficulty cutting—and you're sure your tool is sharp—check the leather to see if it's damp enough. When using a large pattern, it may be necessary to dampen the surface several times as you progress. If there is doubt as to the edge of your cutting tool, sharpen it on an oilstone or strop it on a crocus cloth. Most problems encountered with a swivel knife can be traced to dull blades.

When the design is completely cut, it can be augmented with various stamping tools of your choice. At this point, the leather must look dry on the grain side but remain damp underneath. If necessary, dampen the flesh side with a wet sponge. Be sure to do this or the impression will not take properly. On the other hand, really wet leather will lose its impressions as it dries, so check to see if the stamped impression area looks darker than the leather itself. If it is darker, the leather is at the right degree of dampness.

The first stamping tool generally used on a carved design is the beveler. This tool deepens one side of the outline to make the design itself stand out. The beveler is placed perpendicular to the leather so that its natural slope heads away from the design; the front of the tool rests in the incised outline. Strike the beveler with the mallet and move it along and strike again. This will produce an even impression. As you reach the end of a line, strike the tool with less force so that the beveled part fades out smoothly towards the end.

To add emphasis to the design, use a shader. This tool is also held straight up and down to the working surface and struck with a mallet, as are all stamping tools. The shader can be used anywhere in the design itself and comes in several textures.

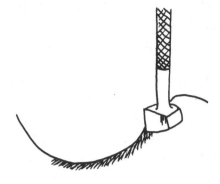

Using a beveler.

Using a shader.

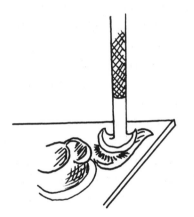

Using a camouflager.

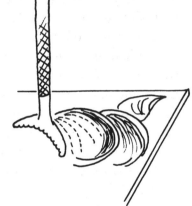

Using a veiner.

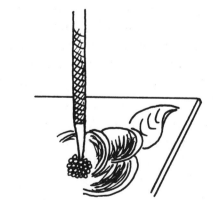

Using a seeder.

90

The camouflager can then be used to add further texture and also to retouch any parts of the design that may need it.

The veiner is used when further accents on leaves and other areas of the design are needed.

When using a seeder, be sure that the centers you stamp are evenly placed and centered for best effect.

As is apparent, the use of stamping tools on a design is governed largely by personal preference. There's no set method or order needed when using several different stampers. Whatever looks best to you is the best thing to do. That's what makes tooling and carving so enjoyable.

Carved patterns can be further decorated, as many are, by using any grounder to produce a textured background in the same way as used on lightweight stamped leather. A border can be added, using any border stamp that appeals to you and your design. The figure stamps, such as flowers and leaves, can also be employed to fill in simple designs. The key to attractive carved leather should be individuality.

TEMPLATES:

When the same design is to be used several times or in the future, a template can be made that will allow for quick transfer of the design without tracing.

The simplest kind of template to make is one constructed of heavy leather—eight to ten ounces in weight. The design is transferred onto the moistened leather from its original paper and carved out with a swivel knife, as it would be carved in any leather. Allow the leather to dry completely. If you want a really long lasting template, dry the leather in a oven set at very low heat—less than two hundred degrees. This will stiffen the leather and deepen the design. Then, coat the dry template with clear lacquer or shellac. Templates can also be etched into aluminum or other non-staining metal or sheet plastic. You can also buy ready made templates from your leather supply shop, these are usually meant for transfer to standard shape items like belts, handbags, wallets or small wall hangings.

To use a template, moisten the leather as you would for tooling. Place the template on the moistened leather so that the design faces the grain side. Use the mallet to transfer the design to the grained surface by pounding the template. Make sure you cover the entire back of the template with blows from the mallet so that the complete design is fully transferred. When finished, the design will be slightly raised when using a home-made template and slightly depressed when applying one that's commercially made. The raised design should be depressed with a modelling tool, then proceed as usual.

BLIND TOOLING:

Blind tooling is a method that uses stamping tools alone to create a border or design. It's a good process to use on bookbindings and can be done on less costly grades of leather with excellent results.

First a pattern is set up—this very often consists of a set of lines, squares or other geometric designs. For example, a plain strap can become an attractive belt with the addition of a stamped row or border along each edge.

The leather to be stamped is moistened with a sponge and the pattern transferred by making very light lines to follow later. Then use whichever stamping tool you've selected to make an even row of impressions that follows the traced lines. A few different stamps can be used to make a design within the pattern.

A similar effect can be created by using an embossing wheel on your project. This tool is applied to moistened leather as in blind tooling.

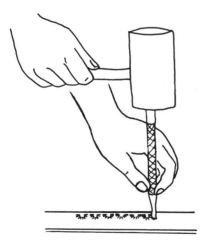

Stamping a border in blind tooling.

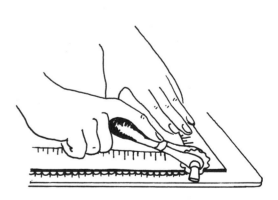

Using an embossing wheel.

It has a wheel that makes a pattern as it's rolled along the surface of the hide. When using the embossing wheel on straight lines, use a ruler as a guide. This tool can also be used to create borders on tooled or carved projects. The wheel itself is exchangeable for any of the many different patterns that are available.

EMBOSSING LEATHER:

This shouldn't be confused with the work produced by the use of an embossing wheel. This is rather a variation of tooled leather. The design itself is accented by making it stand out from the leather like a bas relief. This type of work is most often done on medium weight leathers.

The leather to be embossed is first dampened, allowed to dry a bit and the design traced onto its grain side, just as in all tooling. Deepen the outlines with the modelling tool so that they are visible slightly on the flesh side. Turn the leather over and hold it grain side down in the palm of one hand. Using a ball end modelling tool, go over the inside parts of the design; the pressure of the tool against the leather in your hand will increase the height of the design on the grain side. Be careful and don't attempt to do it all in one sweep or you may push too far into the leather with the tool. The center of the design should stand out the most, so this area can be gone over more than once. While working, look at the grain side once in awhile to check the height of the pushed areas.

Embossing on the flesh side.

When you reach the desired height, turn the leather onto its flesh side and put it on a hard surface. Go over the outlines with the broader end of the modelling tool to make a further contrast between the design and the background. If you'd like, a grounder can be used to fill in the background thereby adding more texture to the design surface. To maintain the height of the embossed areas, wait until the leather has dried completely before proceeding. Then fill the concave parts with small pieces of paper and rubber cement, or make some paste of cornstarch mixed with water and use the paste with pieces of newspaper, like papier mâché, to fill the raised areas. Now let the filling dry and glue a thin leather lining on the flesh side that covers the entire bottom of the design to insure that the filling won't fall out. Your surface will then be permanently embossed.

As tooling and carving is an art, it should be approached as one, with no book fully covering its creative possibilities. However, for those who are truly interested in advance work in this area and feel the need for more detailed instruction before they proceed further or on their own, books devoted entirely to the subject are readily available.

Going over embossed outlines.

Embossed design with papier mâché filler.

CHAPTER NINE

Paints, Dyes and the Finishing Touch

Leather can be beautifully colored with the proper application of suitable paints and dyes. The unique hues and designs achieved are a constant source of pride and individuality.

There are several types of coloring agents that can be successfully applied to leather and suede.

DYES:

Dyes made specifically for use on leather are available in craft stores where leather is sold. They are generally used on natural tan leather, mainly in conjunction with tooled and carved work on cowhide, steerhide and calfskin. There are some types of dye that will cover the colors of other shades of leather, but these are usually opaque and don't allow the natural grain of the hide to show through. Suedes should not be dyed, except for tie dying, as the results are very uncertain and there's a tendency towards fading or uneven coloring.

To color leather that has been carved, it should first be cleaned. Use one of the cleaning fluids available for this purpose, or you can use a

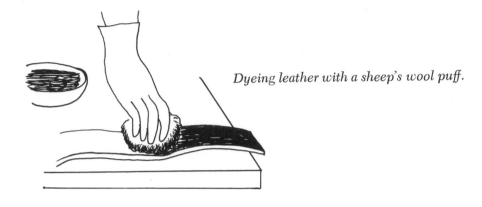

Dyeing leather with a sheep's wool puff.

solution of oxalic acid, made by mixing one tablespoon of acid crystals into one quart of water. This solution is then brushed onto the leather with a sponge. Allow it to dry.

To dye an entire project one color, use a sheeps' wool puff or cheesecloth to spread the dye quickly and evenly across the surface of the leather. Wear rubber gloves to protect your hands. If needed, a second coat of dye can be applied. When using dye for the first time or trying a new color, test the results on a piece of scrap leather identical to the type in the article to be dyed. See how the dye takes and whether the shade produced after the dye is dry is the one you're after. Many of the same name brand dyes can be mixed to blend different colors and thereby make a color or shade of your own. You can also apply one shade on top of another, as long as you've tested with scrap and dye before hand to check results. In any case, when using dye, read the label on the container and follow the manufacturer's instructions for the product.

To dye backgrounds or highlight design parts on carved leather, first clean the surface. Then take a small brush of good quality and dip it into the dye. Keep the brush lightly covered with dye—don't put too much on or the dye will drip or run out onto the leather too quickly. Use short smooth strokes and start in the middle of an area to be dyed, work toward the edges. It's very important to test the dye first to learn how to keep it within the correct color limits. This can only be learned by doing it on scrap first and really shouldn't be tried on a completed article the first time out.

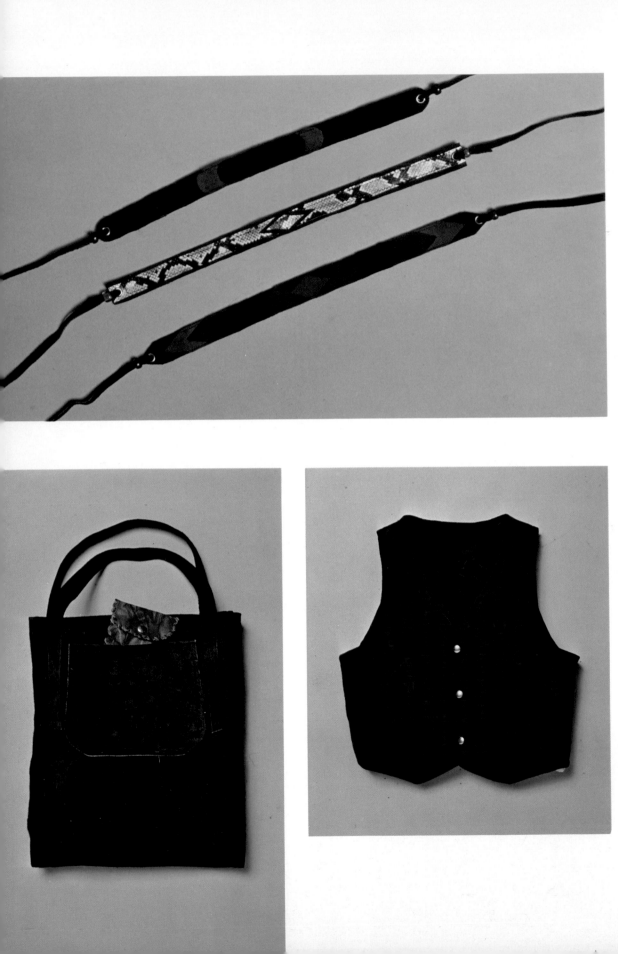

Using opaque dye to completely change the color of a strip of leather.

Another type of dye used for carved or plain leather produces a so-called antique finish, that is, a finish with light and dark highlights of the same color. This dye is applied to dry or slightly dampened leather with a sponge or sheeps' wool puff. The excess dye is removed immediately with a cloth or clean sponge and the remainder allowed to dry. When dry, the entire surface should be rubbed or buffed with a soft cloth or sheeps' wool puff until a light gloss appears on the dyed area. Try it out before commiting your project to this process.

OIL PAINTS:

Regular oil paints can be used on natural color leather to change the color of the entire project or add contrast of color to one small part. When using oil paints on small areas, first prime the leather to prevent the oil from spreading, but this can be a lot of trouble, considering that there are many other color agents available for work in small areas.

To apply oil paints in one shade, clean the leather and allow it to dry throughly. Take a wide brush dipped in thinned paint and apply the paint evenly and in broad strokes. The entire surface should be covered as quickly as possible to avoid streaking. When dry, oil paint allows the natural grain of the hide to show through for interest and highlight.

ACRYLIC PAINTS:

Recently, acrylic paints have leaped into popularity. They are similar to oil paints, but contain some noticeable improvements. The paint is easily washed from hands and brushes with plain water and a little soap perhaps. They're neater and easier to work with on leather as there is no oil to spread to unwanted parts of the surface. The colors are vibrant and work well on all leathers. Acrylics can even be used on suede, for, although they flatten the nap, they produce an unusual effect that should be tried. The main drawback to the use of acrylics is their tendency to obscure the natural grain of the leather.

An interesting way to use acrylics might be to paint a scene of your choice on belts, pocketbooks, shirtbacks or any other article. The paint can be easily applied with a brush and won't run onto the leather as with oils, it also won't blend into another color next to it on the surface. If the paint is too thick, or a more transparent result is what's wanted, there is a medium available for use with acrylics that will thin the paint without the use of water. The medium is milky white and mixes readily with the paint on a palette or plate. Acrylics can also be thinned with water but this won't work as well on leather and isn't advised. When dry, these paints have the great advantage of elasticity, so the painted part of your leather article is unlikely to crack or flake.

STAINS:

Leather stains are sold usually in an oil base solution. They're difficult to use due to their spotty coloring results, matching problems and general unpredictability. By and large, stains are best ignored for the new leathercrafters' work.

FELT TIP PENS:

Felt tip pens are very handy and lots of fun to use. Draw patterns and designs on your leather surface. The pens come in many interesting colors and are simple to control in use. They work well on all light leathers and suedes—the thin lines of color left by the pens don't even obscure the suede nap.

98

DESIGN SET-UP:

A good idea, when choosing a design to paint or print, is to cut a paper model of the project and look at the area to be painted. Will the design fit well? What size is best? A belt can be covered with geometrics or or other shapes, even scenes. A pocketbook can be painted on one large flap, an edge or all over, if the spirit moves you. Draw or trace the design on the paper model. Fill in the planned colors and see what you think. It may take a while longer this way, but the look before you leap method usually pays off. To transfer the design onto the actual leather, use a soft lead pencil or dressmaker's chalk, which can later be brushed off. Or, you can go over an outline by tracing the design onto the underside of the tracing paper with a soft pencil, then turn the paper over again and lay the newly traced line flat to the surface of the leather. Now retrace the drawing on the top side and the pressure will cause the soft pencil lines on the bottom side to adhere and transfer to the leather. Carbon paper can be messy and requires careful use.

USING A STENCIL:

To make a stencil, draw or trace the scene or design onto heavy cardboard or sheet plastic. Keep the scene or design simple for this project so cutting it out isn't too difficult. Cut it out and place the stencil on the leather, hold it in place with one hand. Use acrylic paint or dye that won't run and paint over the entire open area with a brush that isn't overly wet. Now carefully lift the stencil from the surface so that the paint doesn't smear. Let the surface dry. If you'd like, you can add small touches to the dried paint with other colors, for example, if the stencil was in the shape of an animal, you can paint in the eye or other details.

FINISHING LEATHER ARTICLES:

Suedes do not need finishing. All other leathers—except for garment weight cabrettas—should be finished to insure longer life.

Tooled and carved leathers should first be cleaned with the acid solution described under Dyes, or with any commercial leather cleaner.

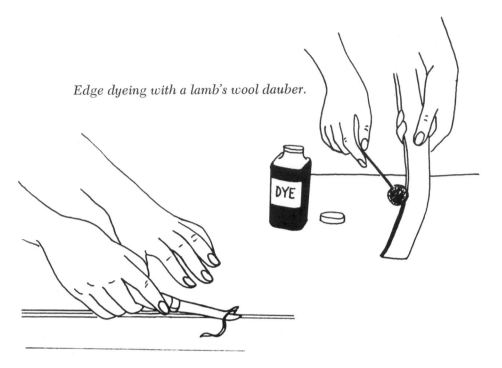

Edge dyeing with a lamb's wool dauber.

Using an edge beveler.

Raw edges should be dyed when necessary. The rough edges of leather, colored or natural, can be attractively finished using leather dye. On heavier leathers, use an edge beveler or other such tool and push it along the edge of the skin to cut off any unevenness and produce a smooth even edge. Edges can also be beveled on leather that isn't being dyed. After beveling, take a felt or lambs' wool dauber and dip it into your dye pot, squeeze the excess dye out and then draw the wet dauber along the raw edge of the leather. Take care not to dye more than the edge itself.

Leather that has been dyed, painted or drawn on with felt tip pens can be finished with clear lacquer. The lacquer can either be sprayed on or applied with a wide brush or sheeps' wool puff. Apply the lacquer smoothly and quickly and try not to go over the same area twice. The best kind of clear lacquer to use is that which is found in leather supply shops. It contains additional ingredients that act as a preservative on leather. Clear lacquer can also be used on natural colored leathers to add sheen as well as a protective coating.

Leather can also be finished using one of the many waxes, pastes and oils specifically made for this purpose. Instructions for their individual use will be found on their containers. It's generally true that they should be applied with a soft cloth or sheeps' wool puff and allowed to dry. If the leather has not been dyed, then buff the dried surface with a soft clean cloth.

Saddle soap is used as a cleaner as well as a preservative and can be applied to leather whenever necessary. It's put on with a damp sponge and rubbed into the surface until a lather forms. If the leather is exceptionally dirty, wipe off the first lather and apply a second. Allow the soap to dry. Then buff the leather with a soft cloth until a natural glow appears on the surface of the skin.

CHAPTER TEN

Make these with Pride-Twelve Complete Plans

The projects in this chapter apply the information and techniques presented in the preceding chapters. Each plan progresses step by step from the materials needed right on through to photographs of the finished articles. It's not difficult and it's fun, so pick a plan and get started. The first article is:

A CHANGE PURSE:

An attractive, useful change purse can be easily constructed from a small amount of leather or suede. It's a good project to begin with and will help you establish a basic knowledge of article design and manufacture.

The purse illustrated is made of tie dyed lambskin, but you can use any supple leather or suede that appeals to you. Whichever material you choose, you'll need a piece measuring one foot long and six inches wide. If the purse is to be sewn instead of laced, your leather can be as small as nine inches long and five inches wide; the lacing takes up more room on the skin.

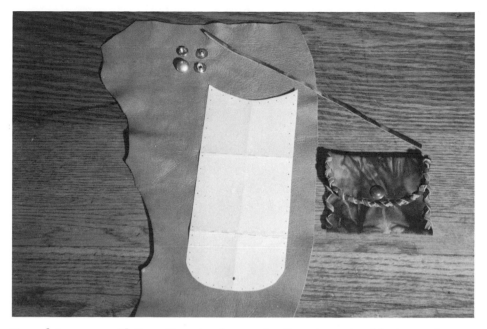

Complete purse with its pattern in place on leather, one strip of lacing and a snap.

Change Purse

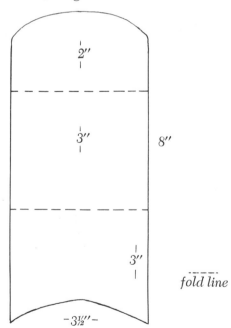

2″

3″

8″

3″

fold line

– 3½″ –

Trace a paper or cardboard replica of the pattern illustrated and cut it out.

Place the cut out pattern close to the long edge on the wrong side of your leather and draw around its outline with a ballpoint pen. Use the remaining leather for lacing if needed by marking strips one-eighth inch wide and as long as possible. For the running or whipstitch, you'll need just about forty-eight inches of lacing; if you prefer the double crossstitch shown, ninety-six inches of lacing will be necessary. The laces can also be bought or made from a contrasting color leather.

Cut out the drawn pattern and laces from the leather with a scissors or craft knife. Use a metal ruler as a guide when cutting with a knife, that will insure straight edges.

Lacing holes should be marked one-quarter inch in from the edge and spaced one-half inch apart. Sewing holes are best one-quarter inch in from the edge and one-quarter inch apart.

Cutting leather with a ruler and knife.

Mark the holes on the flap and middle section only. Then punch the holes out with a rotary or drive punch, or pierce if sewing with an awl.

Fold the third section as indicated and mark through the holes to the unpunched side with a pen. This will insure that they match when you unfold the leather and punch the remaining holes. Mark the rest of the holes on the inwardly curved edge and complete punching.

Begin lacing or sewing on the first hole of the inward curve and lace along the curve. Stop at the last hole after the curve and cut the remaining lace and glue the end on the inside of the seam.

Fold the partially laced and middle sections together to form the body of the purse.

Start to lace at the first double hole after the fold. When doing a single or double cross stitch pull the lace through the holes so that one-half is on each side of the holes. For all other stitches, pull almost all of the lace through and glue the end inside along the holes.

Lace up the side, around the flap and continue down the other side. Splice the lacing when and wherever needed. End by gluing one-half inch of the lace to the inside of the purse along the seam.

If you're sewing the purse together, the instruction remains the same except for the use of a needle and waxed thread in place of the lacing.

Now it's time to set the snap. Mark the bottom half first. Measure one and three-quarter inches in from either edge and three-quarters of an inch down from the inward curve. Punch a hole and set the snap with a snap setting tool and a mallet. Now fold the flap over the set snap bottom and rub the leather over the snap bottom so that an impression is made on the inside of the flap—this will give the exact match needed for the snap to close properly. Punch a hole in the center of the impression created and set the top half of the snap in place. Your first project is now complete.

You can make variations on this design by altering the dimensions of the purse in length, width or both. Change the shape completely if you care to or eliminate the bottom fold by making two parts that are laced together. Two other possible shapes made this way are illustrated. The possibilities are numerous, it's up to you.

If you intend to line the change purse, use the same pattern piece

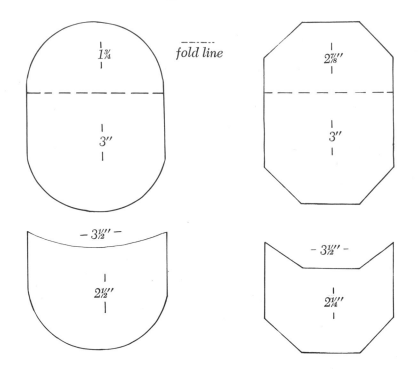

for outline but be sure to cut the lining material one-eighth inch shorter on both top and bottom to allow for the folds. Attach the lining before punching holes, sewing or lacing. Use rubber cement to glue the lining into place in a folded position to avoid wrinkling on the crease lines.

PLUMP PILLOWS:

Pillows add an interesting accent to any room. They're especially attractive when made of colorful supple leathers and suedes. Any lightweight leather or suede material can be used.

The front and back panels of the pillow can match or contrast according to your preference. Almost any combination can be used successfully. The shapes and sizes are subject to almost endless variation but the basic method of making a pillow remains about the same. All you need are some pieces of leather or suede, sewing implements and plenty of stuffing. Shredded foam rubber is particularly suitable and was used in all the pillows illustrated.

To make any shape or size pillow, the basic method is as follows. First mark and cut the leather to the desired specifications. Sew the edges one-half inch in from the edge with the right sides together. Leave about half of one side seam open for turning the pillow right side out to stuff it. If you use a sewing machine, remove the thread from the needle and use the machine to make holes along the remaining unsewn seam—space them as widely as possible. These holes are then used to sew the remaining seam together after the pillow is stuffed.

If you like the effect of raw edges, sew the pillow halves together with the wrong sides touching each other, leave a hole to stuff through and then sew the remaining seam closed. The edges can then be dyed using a dauber. The edges can also be laced using the stitch of your choice.

If you add appliques for contrast and design, do it before making any seams. Just rubber cement the design into place on the right side of the leather or suede and hand or machine sew it on.

The patterns for the pillows shown here are as follows: The first is a simple square shape measuring twelve inches by twelve inches. One side is blue sueded pigskin, the other side is green suede. A five

Front and back panels of a patchwork pillow before sewing.

Open edged pillows after they have been turned right side out and are ready to be stuffed.

inch square applique of the green suede has been glued and sewn to the blue side. The pillow halves were sewn right sides together after the applique was in place—a one-half inch seam allowance was left around the inside edges. A six inch opening was left along one seam and the pillow was turned right side out through this opening and stuffed. The remaining six inches were then sewn by hand, through holes made by the sewing machine needle without thread, prior to turning right side out. It's as simple as that.

The second pillow is made of rust and brown lambskin suede and is in the shape of an elongated hexagon measuring fifteen inches by eleven inches at its longest and widest points. Decorative topstitching can be done on one or both sides before the seams are sewn together. Leave a one-half inch seam allowance and an opening through which to turn the pillow right side out and stuff. Before turning and stuffing, however, remember to make holes along the open seam with a threadless needle if using a machine—or if hand sewing, pierce first for ease of sewing after stuffing.

The third pillow illustrated is a sixteen by fifteen inch rectangular shape made of two colors of lambskin suede. Two strips of each color have been glued and sewn to its contrasting side in a geometric decoration. The strips are one inch wide on one side and one and one-half inch wide on the other. In this case, the strips were crossed near each corner, but they can be placed anywhere you like. The seams on this pillow were made differently from the others and a sewing machine was used. Three sides of the rectangle were sewn, right sides of the suede pressed together, leaving a one-half inch seam allowance and one side of the rectangle open. The pillow was then turned right side out and topstitched along the three sewn seams one-quarter inch in from the edge. The pillow was then stuffed and the remaining open seam was folded one-half inch inwards and topstitched one-quarter inch in from the edge to match the other three sides.

To add a zipper if wanted, place the sewing machine foot along the open seam and sew the zipper in before turning the pillow right side out. The zipper can be taped or rubber cemented into place first to ease handling and sewing.

The front panel of the fourth pillow is made of several types and colors of suede scraps pieced together to form a patchwork design. The pieces can be glued into place with rubber cement on a thin skiver or fabric backing. Then they are zig-zag sewn together after the glue has dried. A sewing machine was used in this design, but larger pieces of patchwork can be hand sewn or laced after gluing. The back panel is made of two matching cowhide split remnants that were glued and sewn together to form one large usable piece. Any color can be used for the back panel or even another piece of patchwork design. As this pillow was made of heavier leather due to the worked pieces, you may choose to sew an outside seam; sew by hand or use a sewing awl. The front and back panels can also be laced together instead of sewn.

CHECKBOOK HOLDER:

Here's a handy and always welcome gift idea; it's a checkbook holder made of fine leather, suede, or snakeskin.

This one is made of python in its natural brown, grey and black hues. The inside is lined and pocketed with brown suede.

The pattern as illustrated calls for one piece of snakeskin measuring about eight inches square, and a foot of suede. Snakeskin is generally long and narrow so it must first be pieced together to form the desired

Finished checkbook cover.

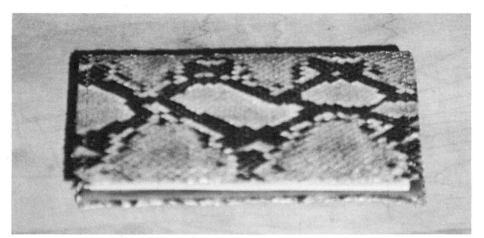

Checkbook Cover

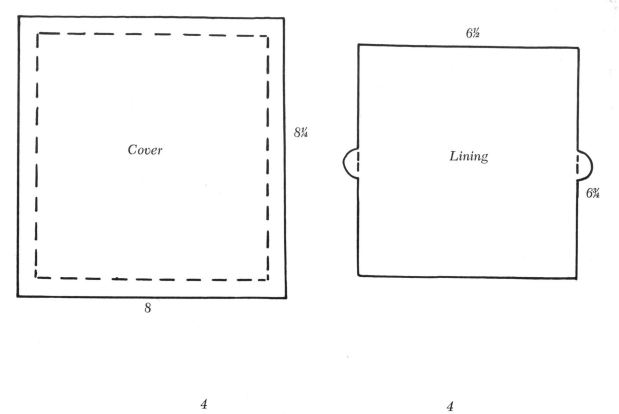

Cover

8

8¼

6½

Lining

6¾

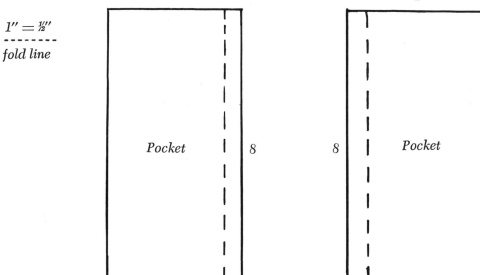

1″ = ½″

- - - - - - -

fold line

4

Pocket

8

4

8

Pocket

square for the cover. This is best done before the pattern piece is cut. If the skin is fairly wide (six inches or so) only one joining or seam will be needed.

First cut the piece of snakeskin in half. The two halves are then glued together along one edge with the right sides pressed together. When the glue has dried, open the skins and fold the glued seam toward one side and topstitch. This creates one wide piece of snakeskin that will accommodate the pattern piece for the outside cover. Now mark the pattern on the inside of the snakeskin square and cut it out. Then mark and cut out the suede lining and two pockets according to the pattern.

Fold under one-half inch on one long edge of each pocket and cement in place. Topstitch it one-quarter inch in from the edge after the glue has dried.

Put the pockets face down with the two seamed edges one and one-half inches apart. Place the lining face down on top of the pockets so that the tabs on either side are between the two pockets. The three unseamed edges of each pocket should extend one-half inch beyond the lining.

Spread rubber cement onto the one-half inch excess, let it get tacky. Then fold it onto the lining and smooth it in place on all sides.

Coat the two tabs lightly with cement, let it get tacky and then fold the two tabs onto the lining and flatten them in place. Turn the lining and the now attached pockets over and allow the cement to dry.

Place the snakeskin cover face down and spread cement one-half inch around the four edges. Fold the edges in one-half inch and flatten them in place gently with a mallet.

Spread cement on one half of the back of the still face-down snakeskin. When the cement is tacky, position the lining and one pocket over the cover and smooth it into place.

Fold the lining and other pocket over the cemented side so that the pockets are on top of each other—just as they'll be when the checkbook cover is closed. Thinly spread cement over the rest of the inside of the face down snakeskin and smooth it into place over the folded lining as if the checkbook holder was now closed. Use the handle of your mallet to smooth the folded parts in place so that the lining doesn't wrinkle.

When the cement dries, topstitch the edges of the pockets and lining to the cover one-eighth inch in from their edges. The same topstitching will come out on the snakeskin cover about one-quarter inch from the edge. This is both decorative and secures the lining to the cover. It's always easier to sew from the inside, however, as you can then be sure that the pocket and lining edges are being included as you sew.

PASSPORT CASE:

As any traveler will tell, a passport case is a useful item to have not only to carry passports, but tickets, health certificates, foreign currencies and other essential items.

If you don't need a passport case, the basic design of this project can be used for a pocket secretary or man's wallet.

The case shown was made and lined with antelope hide, which is a fine skin that can be easily adapted to this and many patterns. However, any thin strong leather or suede can be successfully used.

The pattern as shown consists of six pieces: the cover, lining, and four pockets.

Mark these parts on the wrong side of the leather and cut them out using a craft knife and metal ruler as a guide to obtain straight even edges.

Put the cover face down and cement and fold in a one-half inch edge on all four sides. Spread cement over the entire inside of the cover —excluding the one-half inch folded border.

Position the lining face up over the cover and smooth it into place. As the leather used in this case is very thin, there's little need to worry about wrinkles where the fold occurs. But if wrinkles do appear when folded, undo half of the lining, fold it and re-cement the cover over the fold. Put the lining and cover aside to dry.

Put each of the three rectangular pockets face down and fold a one-half inch seam on one long edge and cement it in place. When dry, topstitch one-quarter inch from the edge.

If you're using laces, make them one-eighth inch wide and lace each folded edge with the holes one-eighth inch in and one-eighth inch apart.

The slanted pocket is folded one-half inch in, first along the slant

Passport Case

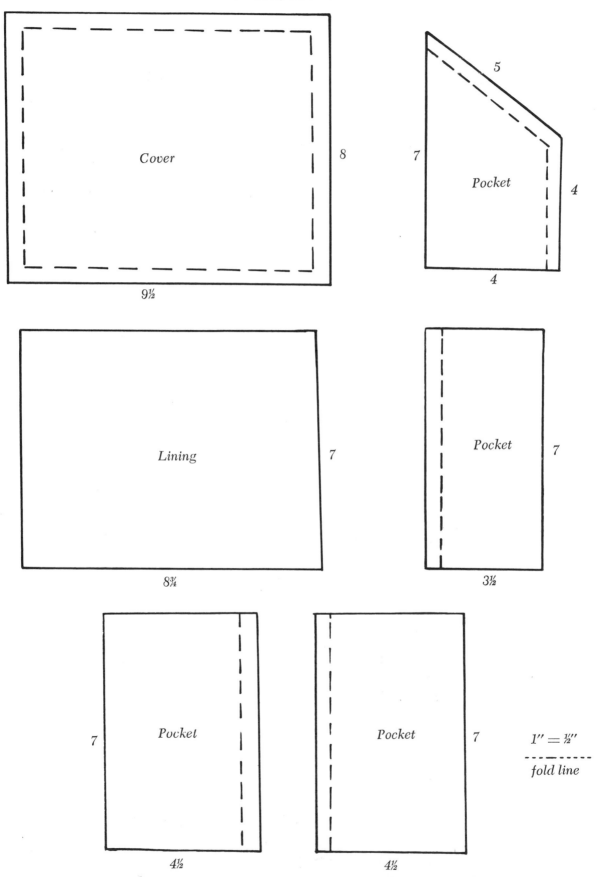

Cover — 8 — 9½

Pocket — 5 — 7 — 4 — 4

Lining — 7 — 8¾

Pocket — 7 — 3½

Pocket — 7 — 4½

Pocket — 7 — 4½

1″ = ½″
------- fold line

edge, then cemented. Then fold and cement one-half inch in along the edge of the same side on which the slant occurs. Topstitch or lace along the slanted edge only.

Take one of the two larger pockets and put it face up. Put the slanted pocket face up on top of it so that its two raw edges meet two edges of the pocket beneath. The slanted pocket will extend up to the seam on the edge of the other pocket but should not cover it. Sew or lace the slanted pocket onto the other pocket along the one edge indicated.

Place the cover face down so that the lining is face up. Spread cement on one-quarter inch on the wrong side of the three raw edges of each large pocket. Position each pocket over the lining one-eighth inch from the edge of the cover. The last pocket, the narrow rectangular one, is then spread with cement one-quarter inch on the wrong side and glued over the plain large pocket so that their two seamed edges are one-quarter inch apart and their raw edges meet.

The entire case is then stitched or laced one-fourth inch from the

Inside of the passport case.

edge on all four sides. The stitches or laces should go over all raw edges, pockets and lining to secure all the cemented parts. Although you're stitching on the inside, make certain that the outside stitches are attractive as they become the topstitching for the outside cover. When lacing, you can work from either side as long as you're sure all edges have been included in the lacing holes.

WRITING SECRETARY OR LEGAL SIZE PAD HOLDER:

For stationery, writing pads and envelopes, an attractive cover can be made of any sturdy leather or heavyweight cowhide split. The cover illustrated was made of sueded pigskin with cowhide split binding, lacing and lining. The combination of these two four-ounce leathers allows for strength and long wear. If you intend to use a lighter weight leather for the article, a stiffener like cardboard or thin plastic should be inserted between the cover and the lining. This cover was made to fit a legal size pad but can easily be altered to any size pad you wish by changing the dimensions accordingly.

The basic pattern as illustrated is made of six pieces and consists of two front and back panels of pigskin, a binding, lining and pocket of cowhide and a piece of heavy scrap leather to reinforce the slit through which the back of the pad fits into the holder. The lacing needed for the whipstitch shown is about ten feet long and a quarter inch wide and is cut from the same cowhide as the lining and pocket.

The material needed is two feet of pigskin and four feet of cowhide—or six feet of the leather of your choice.

Set up a paper pattern, mark and cut the pieces using a knife and metal ruler to maintain straight edges.

The first step after cutting is to sew the binding to the front and back panels. Fold a one-half inch seam along each long edge of the binding. Rubber cement the seam in place and pound it flat with a mallet. Then cement the binding in place on the two panels one-half inch from their edges to form a lapped seam. Sew the binding into place with topstitching one quarter-inch in from the folded binder edge. Use an awl, sewing machine or needle and thread. If you're using a sewing machine, insert the heaviest weight leather needle and use silk or polyester core thread.

To prepare the lining, glue a strip on the wrong side where the split for the pad back is to be made and topstitch it into permanent position on the right side of the lining.

Measure and cut the slit with a knife and metal ruler after sewing.

Fold a one-half inch seam on the top of the pocket, cement and pound with a mallet. Topstitch the pocket one-quarter inch from the folded edge.

Legal Size Pad Holder

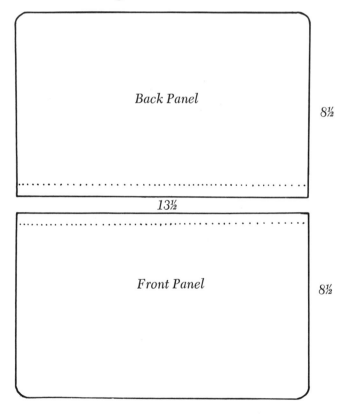

Back Panel

8½

13½

Front Panel

8½

1″ = ½″
- - - - - - - - -
binding line

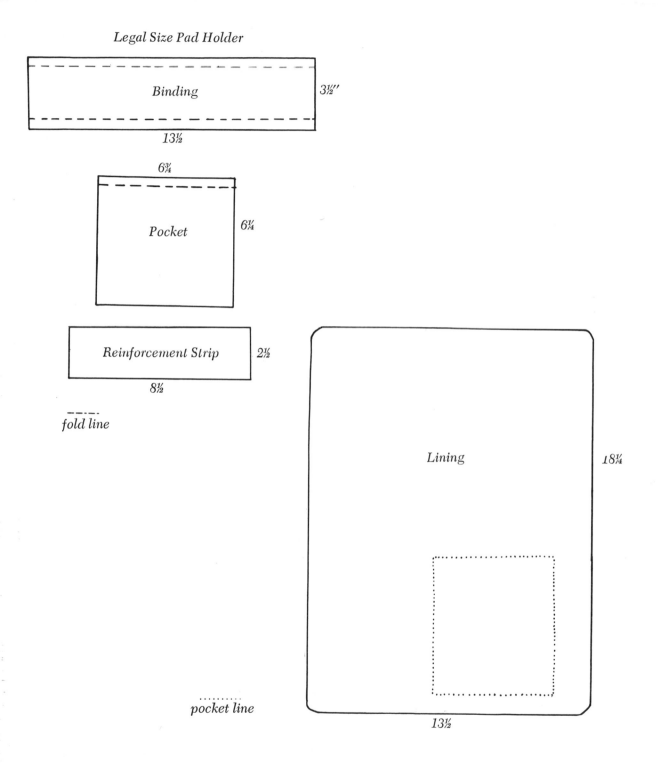

Legal Size Pad Holder

Binding

3½″

13½

6¾

Pocket

6¼

Reinforcement Strip

2½

8½

fold line

Lining

18¼

pocket line

13½

Apply a thin coat of cement, one half inch wide, on the wrong side of the remaining three edges and glue the pocket onto the right side of the lining. Make two rows of topstitching to secure the pocket in place—one right at the edge and the other row one-quarter inch in from the edge. The lining is now ready to put into place on the cover.

Spread cement on the front half of the cover and pocket half of the lining. Smooth in place up to the fold line in the center of the cover. Fold the lining in half so that its right edges meet as they should when the cover is closed. Spread cement on the fold of the lining and one-half inch around the edges of the rest. Cement the inside cover where the fold will occur and one-half inch around the edges—don't glue the rest of the lining to the cover as the pad back must fit through the slit and rest between the lining and the cover.

Fold the outside cover over the folded lining and smooth the folded parts together with the rounded handle of the mallet so that the lining doesn't wrinkle when the cover is closed. Pat the edges together and allow to dry completely.

Mark holes for lacing on the outside cover and space them one-half inch from the edge and one-half inch apart.

At the corners, make the holes a bit closer together. Use a ruler and pen or a stitch gauge to mark the holes.

Punch the holes out with a mallet and drive punch or a rotary punch.

Since it's difficult to fit the lacing between the cemented lining and the cover, the laces are started and ended in a different way than usual. Pull the lace through the first hole and leave one-half inch of lace loose on the inside of the cover. Lace around the cover—go twice into each corner hole—use the whip stitch and splice the lace where necessary until you return to the starting hole.

Cut the lace with a tapering tip so that it will cover the one-half inch lace you left sticking out when you started.

Apply rubber cement to the underside of the last lace piece and the top side of the first end.

Smooth the last lace piece over the first lace end so that the tapered tip goes part way into the first lace hole. The finished lace will then look continuous with no obvious joining.

Lightly pound the finished laces with a mallet to flatten them to the cover.

Lacing the writing pad holder.

Cementing the last lace under side and first end top side.

Smoothing the last lace end over the first lace end.

Flattening the finished laces to the cover with a mallet.

A BEVY OF BELTS:

Belts are such a traditional use of leather that no leather book would really be complete without them—besides, they're enjoyable to design and make as well as practical. Make them wide or narrow, plain or fancy—here are several to choose from:

The first belt illustrated here was given a Western flavor by the use of stamping tools. It's one and a half inches wide and is made of eight ounce carving leather stamped with a random design and dyed.

You can either cut a strip of belt to the desired width and length from a hide or buy blank strips of leather specifically cut for this purpose. Whichever you choose, here's what to do.

If you're cutting strips yourself, use a draw gauge knife or a craft knife and ruler—the heaviness of the leather used in the Western type belt makes cutting with a scissors just about impossible. When the strip is cut, shape both ends to form ovals or slightly rounded ends—from here on the instruction is the same whether you're buying blanks or cutting your own.

Burnish the raw edges of the strip with a wide modeller or bevel with an edge tool.

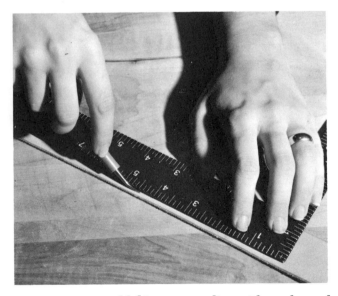

Making a creaseline with a ruler and basic modelling tool.

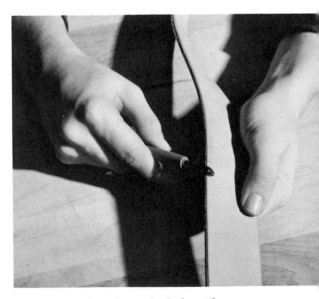

Burnishing the edges of a belt with the broad end of a tool.

Moistening leather with a sponge.

Using stamping tools on a moistened belt strip.

To prepare for stamping or carving, moisten the leather as described in Chapter Eight and make a crease line one-eighth inch from all edges —use a ruler and a basic modelling tool or an edge creaser.

Moisten the leather again if necessary and begin to stamp the design you've chosen. The stamps used on this belt were of three different but harmonious patterns applied with no set pattern. You can, of course, choose any stamp to apply a free or set design.

After stamping, the design of this belt was daubed briskly with a thin coat of cordovan brown dye. A thin coat was used so that the impressions made by the stamping tools were not filled and retain their natural color in contrast to the dye.

To fit a buckle, set two snaps one inch apart on the desired end of the belt so that the buckle is removable and may be used for other belts as well. Cut a slot between snap bottoms and tops to fit the tongue of your buckle through. Then snap the buckle into place. This particular belt buckle is designed to create its own holder, but if your buckle requires a holder to keep the rest of the belt in place after closing, cut a one-half inch strip of leather and form it into a flattened rectangle to fit around the belt. Secure the ends together by sewing. The holder is then slipped between the two snaps and is held in place by them when the buckle is attached.

Measure the holes for the belt closure according to the waist size of the wearer and mark them on the wrong side of the leather. Punch the holes and set them with eyelets or grommets for long life. To be on the safe side for most people, it's a good idea not to make the size too exact, a hole or two on either side of the size allows for a slight fluctuation in waist measurement.

The second belt is made of heavy sueded cowhide split and is two inches wide. First cut the leather strip and round off the ends.

Topstitch two rows for either decoration or to secure a lining or both. Make the first rows one-eighth inch from the edges and the second rows one-half inch in. Cut a slot for the buckle tongue and set the buckle in place. Cut a one-half inch wide keeper and after sewing the ends together, slip it onto the belt behind the buckle.

Set four rivets, two in front of the keeper and two behind it to secure the keeper and the buckle at the same time. Of course, if you prefer to change buckles or belts you can attach them with snaps as in the first belt so they'll be removable.

Set decorative spots or studs all the way around the belt directly in the center, or in two rows, each a half inch from the edges and an inch apart. Smaller spots can also be applied between the two rows of stitching if desired.

Punch holes for grommets or eyelets along the same line as the studs to give an overall design and set them into place.

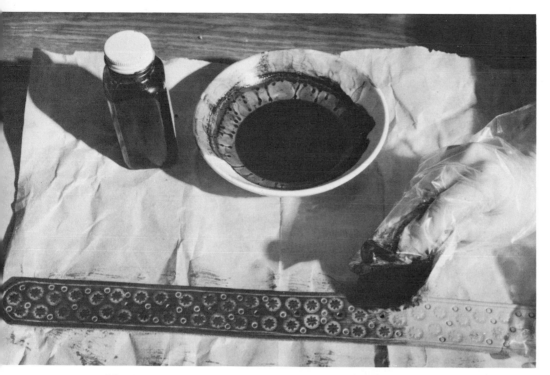

Briskly dyeing a tooled belt with a lamb's wool puff.

Setting eyelets in a studded belt.

An interesting way to use scraps and other leather odds and ends is to combine them and make a patchwork belt. The belt shown is four inches wide. First a lining of light to medium weight leather or suede should be cut to the needed length and width. The patchwork pieces can then be arranged on the lining and cemented to it. The patches here were zig-zag stitched together and then top stitched.

A patchwork belt with the materials used to make it.

Design created by Gene Narmore.

Two cloverleaf pattern belts and cardboard pattern.

124

A finished overlapping pattern belt and materials (two views).

The fastening of this belt is made with eight eyelets placed so that the belt can be laced together with one-quarter inch wide suede strips in place of a buckle.

Another way to use small pieces of leather is to make an overlapping pattern of the design illustrated. The basic idea is to cut panels with one shaped end and overlap them one over the next to form a belt. These are all three inches wide, and mostly made of sueded cowhides.

Among the many shapes that can be used are the abstract clover-leaf, zig-zag or the rounded edge designs shown.

Use a cardboard or heavy paper pattern as shown. This pattern is cut out of leather as many times as needed to make a belt of the desired length. This is measured by totaling the length of each panel minus the shaped end and adding them together for a total length. The center panel is cut smaller than the rest by drawing the end shape once, turning the pattern around and drawing the shape one inch away to create the other end of the center piece.

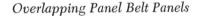

Overlapping Panel Belt Panels

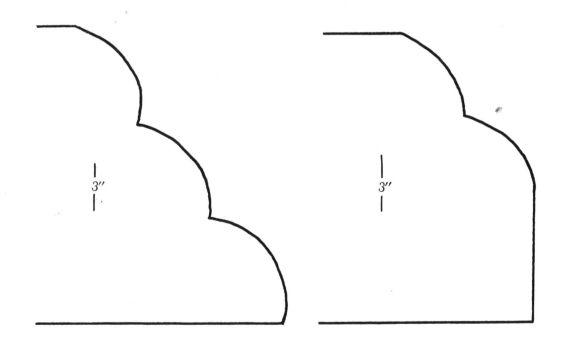

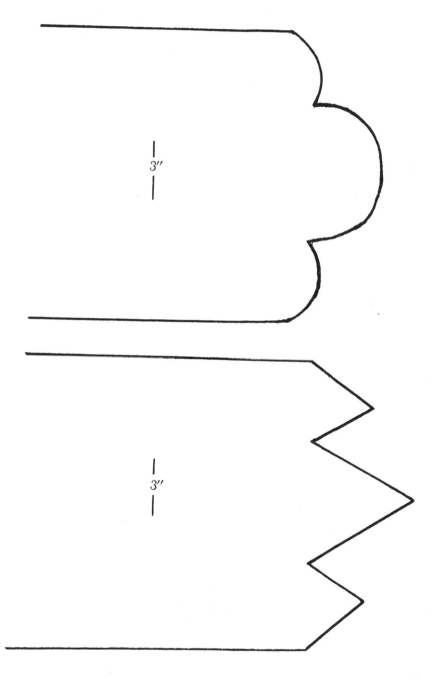

3″

3″

After the panels are cut, apply rubber cement to the wrong side of one panel on the shaped end only. Fit this end over the straight edge of the next panel and smooth it into place. Continue until half the panels have been used. Then make another series of panels for the other side of the belt. Place these two strips so that the two straight ends are next to each other and fit the smaller center portion over the straight edges to join both halves of the belt.

Cut a strip of leather or suede for use as a lining and use the paper pattern to shape the ends so that they fit the shaped front ends of the belt.

Cement the two end panels to the lining and stitch the rest in place one-quarter inch from the edge. Continue the stitches around the shaped ends, turn and go up the other side to stitch that shaped end.

These belts are fastened with one-quarter inch strips attached through eyelets on the tip of each end. This type of belt could also be fastened with a buckle by extending the end panel on each side to accommodate the buckle and holes.

Marking a panel for a zig-zag pattern belt on leather.

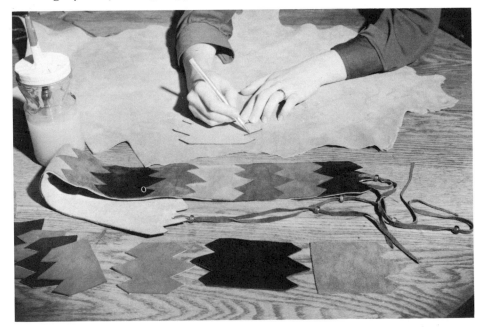

Rubber cementing a zig-zag pattern belt.

Putting a cemented panel in place on a zig-zag pattern belt.

Chokers made from scraps of leather using the same method as the overlapping pattern belt.

129

Any type of leather, suede or snakeskin can be used in combination on these belts with truly lovely results.

Belts of this type, without buckles, were originally designed and created by the author and were sold out in a leading high fashion department store in New York for over thirty dollars each.

The use of acrylic paints on leatherwork can achieve very satisfying results as when applied to the following belt. The body of the belt is four inches wide with a lining cut to match and the same laced closing as described in the patch and overlapping belts.

There is a row of stitches one-quarter inch from each edge for decoration and attachment of the lining. The stitches should be made before eyelets or grommets are set into place.

The design is then painted on the finished belt. You can also paint the leather before creating the belt if you prefer. The design chosen can be done either on parts of the belt or the entire surface, according to the effect that pleases you most.

You may sometimes come across an antique or other unusual buckle that really should be put on a belt and worn, but somehow just doesn't seem to work the way you'd expect it to.

That was the case with the belt shown here. A piece was missing from the back of the buckle and the two tongues were soldered in place so they did not move. The solution was found with the use of a modern two pronged belt hook, three rivets and a couple of snaps. The leather of the belt is heavy brown cowhide weighing about eight ounces. This is the way to solve the problem:

Cut or buy the belt strip of the desired width, in this case, one and one-half inches. Measure and cut for length, leaving two extra inches on both ends. Dye the cut edges if necessary. Skive about two inches along either end or pound vigorously with a mallet.

Most antique buckles have a few bars along the back to fit the belt fabric into. Using the extreme left bar, slip the buckle onto the belt for about two inches.

Set a snap bottom at the end of the two inch piece and a snap top on the body of the belt. Another snap bottom can be placed an inch away on the strip for size adjustment of the belt around the wearer's waist.

On the other end, fold two inches and cut a slit into the fold large

A belt finished with a design done using acrylic paints.
Design created and executed by Olga Ley.

Dyeing the slit for a two pronged hook on a belt with an antique buckle.
Shown with rivets and a rivet setting tool.

enough for the two prongs of the hook to fit snugly through. Dye the slit edges if needed.

Fit the two prongs into the slit hook side up. Mark through the holes in the belt hook with a ballpoint pen to mark the two inch strip for rivets.

Punch holes where marked and set three small rivets through the belt hook and into the leather beneath.

At the end of the two inch strip, set a snap bottom. Set a snap top on the outside of the belt. Although this snap opens and closes as with any other, its main purpose is to decorate the belt by providing balance to the snap on the other side.

THE SUEDE SACK:

This is a handy tote bag for those days when you're marketing or have to carry several items. There's even a handy outside pocket for easy-to-reach items like keys, your purse or even a newspaper. The pattern is simple and straight; it's a large rectangle that's easily fashioned into a useful article.

This one is made of shaggy reversible split cowhide. The inside of the skin is a rough suede with lots of hairy nap. The outside is the more usual sueded cowhide. This sack can also be made of any other split cowhide or medium weight leather that's durable and resistant to stretching. Since the leather used is of fairly heavy weight, it's not necessary to line this bag but you can do so if you like.

You'll need about six square feet of leather. Make certain that the skin you choose will accommodate a thirty-four by sixteen inch rectangle.

The other pattern pieces are for one outside pocket and two sturdy strap handles. Make your copy of the paper pattern, mark it on the wrong side of the leather by drawing around its outline and cut it out.

Make the pocket by folding under one inch of leather along the longest straight edge. Cement the fold into place and pound lightly with your mallet. When the glue is dry, topstitch the hem of the pocket three-eighths of an inch in from the folded edge.

Spread a thin coat of cement one-half inch around the three remaining edges of the pocket. When tacky, glue the pocket in place where indicated on one side of the right side of the leather rectangle.

132

The seamed edge of the pocket should be two and a half inches from the top edge of the rectangle. Sew the three unseamed edges in place using two rows of stitching for added strength; the first row should be right at the edges of the pocket and the second row about three-eighths of an inch further in. Start the stitching at one corner; when

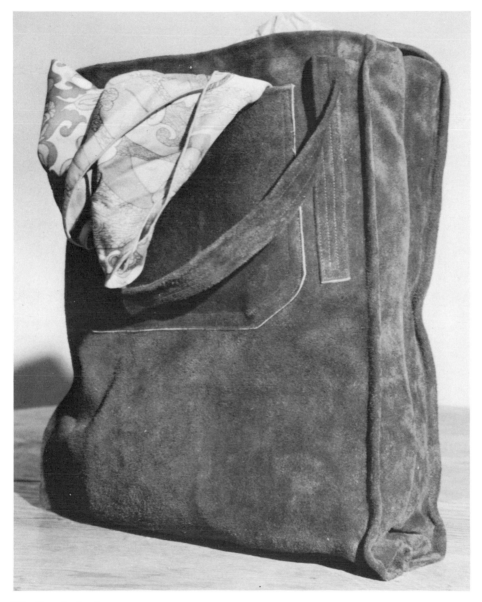

The Suede Sack.

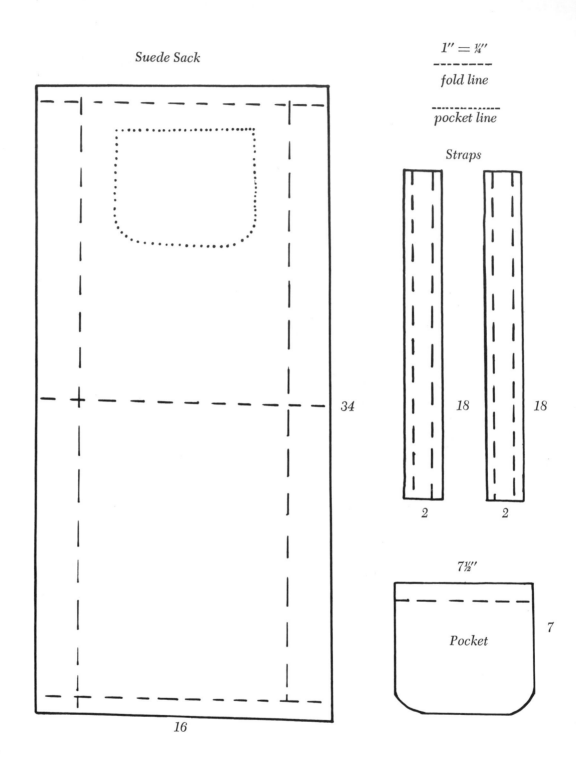

Suede Sack

$1'' = \frac{1}{4}''$

------- fold line

.... pocket line

Straps

34

18   18

2   2

$7\frac{1}{2}''$

Pocket   7

16

134

you reach the other corner, turn, stitch in from the edge for the second seam, turn and go back to the other corner, turn and make a few stitches up to the first stitch, pull all the thread ends in to the wrong side of the leather and tie them off.

Fold one inch to the wrong side along each short end of the rectangle, cement in place and flatten with a mallet. Topstitch three-quarters of an inch in from the edge.

Fold the rectangle in half, right sides together. Make a seam along the fold line by sewing one-half inch in and reinforce the seam with a second row of stitches about three-eighths of an inch in from the edges.

Take each strap strip and spread it with cement on the wrong side. Fold in one-half inch on each long edge. Pound with a mallet to flatten and top stitch one-quarter inch in from each fold.

Use cement to put strap handles in place on the right side of the pocket side. One end of the strap should be on each side of the pocket with the inner strap edge running parallel one-half inch away from the pocket edge. The tip of the strap ends six inches away from the top seamed edge of the rectangle.

Place the other strap on the right side of the other half of the rectangle in the same position. The inner edges of the strap handles on this side are parallel to each other about eight inches apart. Secure the straps with topstitching right at the edges, around the bottom tip and across the strap at the top seam line. A second set of stitches within the first, placed one-quarter inch away, will insure a sturdy strap.

Put the rectangle face up. There are now straps on each end and a pocket on one side; the edges are seamed and there's a folded seam along the center.

Working along each of the two unfinished edges, fold two and a half inches in on each side and topstitch, one-quarter inch in from the fold. You can ease the sewing by cementing the one-half inch of the fold on the wrong side before starting to stitch.

Put the right sides together and fold in half so that the stitched seam forms the bottom and the two straps are together at the top. Stitch one-half inch in along the two outside edges and put another row of stitches one-quarter inch in for added strength.

Turn the bag right side out and your Suede Sack is ready for toting.

POUCH POCKETBOOKS:

Pocketbooks can be made in all shapes and sizes following the basic technique. The pocketbook shown is a simple rounded pouch with a flap and shoulder strap handle. If you prefer a shorter handle, just alter the pattern piece before cutting.

The pattern used here was adapted from an existent pocketbook. You can either copy, enlarge or alter this pattern or create one of your own following the instruction in Chapter Four. There are also quite a few patterns available at leathercraft shops.

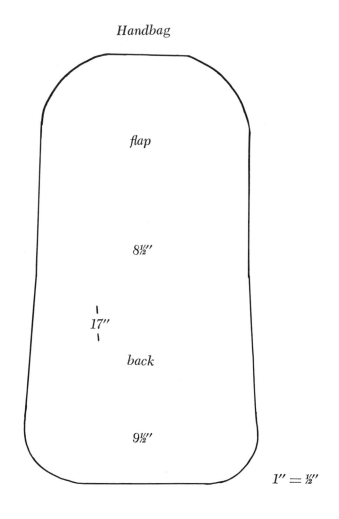

Handbag

flap

$8\frac{1}{2}''$

$17''$

back

$9\frac{1}{2}''$

$1'' = \frac{1}{2}''$

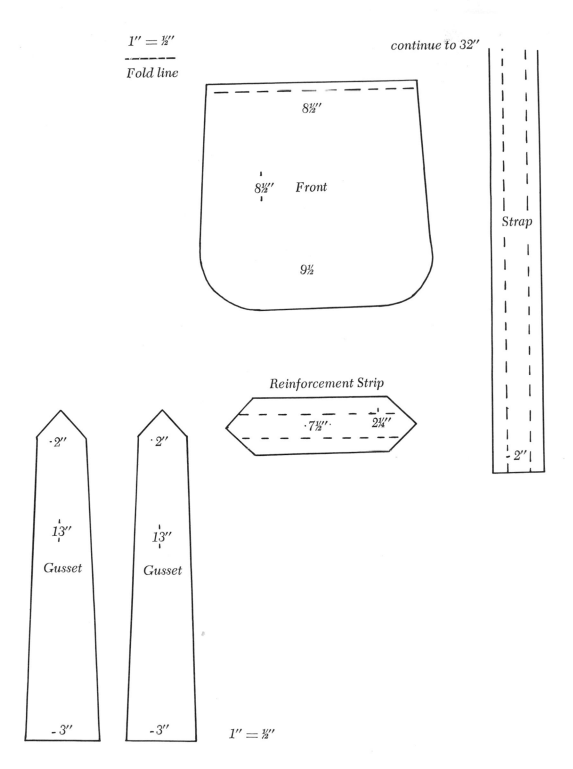

$1'' = \frac{1}{2}''$

Fold line

$8\frac{1}{2}''$

$8\frac{1}{2}''$ Front

$9\frac{1}{2}$

continue to 32''

Strap

$2''$

Reinforcement Strip

$\cdot 7\frac{1}{2}'' \cdot$ $2\frac{1}{4}''$

$\cdot 2''$

$\cdot 2''$

$13''$

$13''$

Gusset

Gusset

$- 3''$ $- 3''$

$1'' = \frac{1}{2}''$

137

Making a pattern from a pocketbook.

This bag is made of lambskin suede, but any lightweight suede or leather can be used. Heavier leathers are also suitable, especially if the seams are to be laced, sewn by hand or with a sewing awl.

This pattern calls for about six square feet of leather. If you want to line the bag, you'll need five more feet of a lightweight lining leather or fabric. You'll also need six small rivets and a rivet setting tool.

Make a paper pattern. Mark and cut out all the parts on the wrong side of your leather. The six parts are: the back of the bag and flap, the front, two gussets, the strap, and a reinforcement piece for the strap center. If the length of the strap is too long for your piece of leather, make it in two equal pieces.

To line the pocketbook, cut a duplicate of the back, front and gussets from the lining material using the same pattern pieces as your guide.

Sew the gussets together at the bottom seam to form one continuous strip—leave a one-half inch seam allowance. Do the same for lining gussets, if used. Flatten the seam allowance and rubber cement in place.

With the right sides together, fit the gusset strip around the back bottom section of the bag; leave one and three-quarter inch of the top of each gusset free from the seam. Use a cellophane or masking tape to hold in place and sew together with a half inch seam allowance. When sewing by machine, a second row of stitches near the first will strengthen the attachment.

138

Sew the lining pieces together as a separate unit in the same fashion.

Fold one-half inch under along the straight edge of the front panel and topstitch. Fit the panel to the gusset, tape in place and sew. Do the same for the lining.

Clip small V-shaped notches around the curved parts of the flap, make them one-quarter inch at their deepest point. Use cement to hold in place as you fold in one-half inch around the flap to create a flat seam. Do the same for the lining flap.

You now have two separate pocket book shapes. Turn the pocketbook right side out. Leave the lining as it is and fit it into the bag. Use rubber cement to secure the lining in place and topstitch one-quarter inch in from the edge around the entire flap. Do a second row of stitching along the straight edge of the front of the bag.

The tops of the gusset on each side now extend one and three-quarter inches above the edge of the front of the bag. Fold the seam allowances and cement in place so that the remaining strip is one inch wide and one and three-quarter inches tall. Do the same for the lining.

Spread the strap with a thin coat of cement and fold one-half inch in on each long edge. The reinforcement strip is then cemented in the center of the strap, with one-half inch folded around and in to cover the strap itself. Topstitch each long edge one-quarter inch in.

If the strap was cut in two pieces, sew them together at the end of each part; the reinforcement strip will cover the joining seam.

Fit each end of the strap in between the one and three quarter inch gusset strips of the pocketbook and lining. Cement in place. If you're not using a lining, cement the gusset strip on the outside of the strap for one and three-quarter inches. Topstitch a rectangle within the one and three-quarter inches of the gusset strip and glued strap.

Punch two holes for rivets within the stitched rectangle—make the holes three-quarters of an inch apart. Set one rivet in each hole. Punch a hole and set another rivet at each end of the reinforcement piece on the strap one-half inch in from the end of the reinforcement and one-half inch in from its edges.

To lace the same pocketbook; trim all one-half inch seam allowances to one-quarter inch. Sew the gusset bottoms together. Cement the wrong side of the lining to the wrong side of each pocketbook section to be lined.

Setting a rivet in place to join handbag strap and gusset.

Setting a rivet.

Punch lacing holes one-quarter inch apart and one-quarter inch in from the edges. Hold the seams together with cement if desired and lace from the outside—follow the same steps as for the sewn pocketbook.

The handle can be sewn or laced. If it is laced, follow the same steps as in sewing, except lace the strap to the gussets after they are glued together. The laced bag doesn't really need rivets, but they can be added for extra strength and decoration.

TWO VESTS FOR WOMEN:

A suede or leather vest is a versatile addition to anyone's wardrobe. Vests aren't difficult to make and are useful, attractive and long lived.

The first vest shown is a simple waist length design and is made of purple sueded cowhide. The pattern used for this vest was purchased— it's Simplicity's number 9300.

You'll need about ten square feet of leather or suede. Bring the pattern with you when you go to buy your leather; lay it out on the skin or hide at the shop to make certain the piece is large enough.

The lining is made of black taffeta—you'll need about seven-eighths of a yard.

In this case a longer vest was desired so the pattern was lengthened one and one-half inches on all its parts before it was cut.

To cut, lay out the pattern on the skin with the indicated grain line of the pattern following the backbone of the animal. Tape the pieces in place to ease cutting and use heavy duty scissors or leather shears. Remember to make a right and left back by turning the pattern over after cutting the first piece—this is done because patterns are made for cutting on folded material—a practice not recommended for use with leather.

After cutting, mark seam lines and darts on the wrong side of your leather with a tracing wheel and chalked paper, or use a ballpoint or felt tip pen.

Cut out the lining as indicated, on folded taffeta. Mark the back of each lining piece with the tracing wheel and paper or dressmaker's chalk.

Sew the vest together, following the instructions on the pattern sheet. Press open all seams with your fingers and cement them in place.

Cut pattern parts for waist length vest with sewing awl.

Cut open darts, cement and flatten. Pound all seams lightly with a mallet.

The lining is sewn separately. The two parts, vest and lining, are then sewn, right sides together.

The space indicated for turning the vest right side out should be left open along the left front seam for at least three or four inches. The extra length of this opening is due to the bulkiness of leather—as this particular pattern was not specifically designed for use with leather or suede. After turning, be sure all corners and seams are completely extended before closing the seam.

Once the vest is right side out, the seam along the opening is folded inwards and topstitched in place one-quarter inch from the edge. The rest of the edges are also topstitched at the same distance from the edge.

Three snap fasteners are applied at evenly spaced distances from each other. Punch three holes on the left side to set the snap bottoms first. Then, mark for snap tops by putting the vest in a closed position. Feel where the snap bottoms are and make a dot on the leather in the center of each. This will insure alignment of the snap parts for proper closing.

Punch a hole at each dot and set the snap tops. Any number of snaps can be used; it's up to you.

The second vest is made of tan reversible cowhide, suede side out. You'll require about fifteen square feet of material. This vest was made using McCall's pattern number 2454. However, the tied lace closure indicated in the original pattern was replaced by two large galoshe type fasteners and the lining was omitted.

The pattern parts are taped in place and cut out of the leather. Sew all seams according to directions—ignore the references to the lining. Cement and flatten all the seams.

Finish the raw edges by spreading cement on seam allowances. Fold allowances in and pound with mallet.

Wherever there are curved parts, cut V-shaped notches within the seam allowance to permit flat cementing. Do the hem in the same manner using rubber cement to hold in place. Topstitch all edges, including armholes.

To apply the fasteners, cut four strips of leather one and three-quarter inches wide and four inches long. Spread cement on the wrong side of each strip and fold in one half inch on each long edge. Slip each

Setting snap fasteners in a vest.

Flattening a seam on a vest.

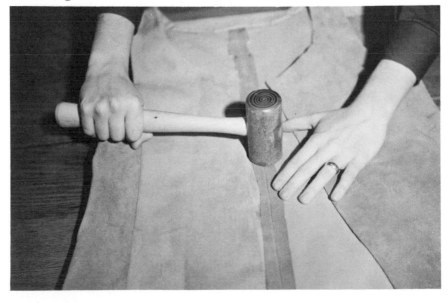

strip into the end of each part of the fasteners until the fastener is on the center of the strip. Cement the strip ends together. Cement each folded strip and fastener onto the vest with loop ends on the left side and hooked ends on the right. Put one at the top of the vest and one at the waist. Top stitch in place.

If you're going to lace a vest, make the seam allowance one-quarter inch instead of the usual five eighths, mark and punch holes as previously described in Chapter Five and lace it up.

MAKING A SKIRT:

Leather skirts are smart and wearable and seem always to stay in fashion even while other styles change rapidly.

The skirt illustrated here is a A-line with a yoked front. Any skirt with similar A-line or slightly flared shape will work well in leather and suede. It's a good idea to avoid full or pleated skirts as their designs aren't really suitable for the fall and drape qualities of the leather materials.

The pattern used for this skirt is McCall's number 2545. The skirt is made of reversible cowhide split in a dark warm brown color. Although the directions are given for this particular skirt's construction, they will apply equally well as a guide to the making of any skirt.

To make this type of skirt, you'll require about eighteen square feet of garment cabretta, suede or light to medium weight cowhide split. Take the pattern along to the leather shop when buying your material. You'll also need about a yard of taffeta lining and a seven inch skirt zipper or other fastener.

Buy the pattern that suits you. To get the right size, measure at the hip and waist and choose the size closest to these measurements. Of course, it's possible that you won't find a pattern size that matches your measurements exactly. In that case, buy the next larger size as it's easier to make things smaller according to your needs. Remember, leather clothing can be taken in simply enough, but can't really be let out.

To adjust the pattern to size before cutting your leather, each major piece can be cut apart. Notice the grain line marking and cut parallel to it to increase by adding tissue or decrease evenly. If one inch has to be added or removed from four major pieces, take one-quarter inch from each section. To lengthen or shorten a skirt, printed instructions are given on pattern pieces.

When all adjustments have been made, you're ready to cut the skins. Lay pattern parts on the right side of the leather and tape in place. Don't forget to make the second half of all parts usually cut on folded fabric—turn the pattern face down for the second half and leave a five-eighths inch seam allowance at the original fold line. Or, you can cut a paper replica of the second half, tape both halves of the pattern together at the fold line and then cut as one. If the hide isn't large enough to accommodate one large pattern part, it can be pieced by cutting apart at a logical place and adding a five-eighths inch seam allowance on each cut piece.

Cut out all parts. Mark darts and other sewing information on the wrong side with chalked paper and a tracing wheel, or use a ballpoint or felt tip pen.

145

Using a tracing wheel and chalked paper to mark sewing information on the wrong side of cut leather.

Sew the skirt together, following the steps described on the pattern and flatten the seams. If there is no waistband, use an inner waistband of one and one-half inch wide grosgrain ribbon or belt backing.

The zipper is put in with a centered application. Use tape to hold the zipper in place instead of trying to baste it. Full instructions for zipper application are found inside each zipper package.

The lining is sewn together as a separate unit and attached at the waistband.

The skirt hem is cemented in place and lightly pounded on the inside to flatten it a bit. If the inner hem bunches, cut out the extra leather using V-shaped notches.

If necessary, press the completed skirt with a warm iron and heavy paper or cloth between the leather and the iron. Don't use steam as it can stain leather permanently.

To lace a skirt instead of sewing, trim the seam allowances to one-quarter inch, and mark and punch lacing holes. The punched parts are then placed side by side and laced together with the stitch of your choice.

A MAN'S VEST:

Leather vests are just as useful and attractive for men and boys as they are for women. Sturdy leathers in deep tones are especially suitable.

The vest shown is made from heavy cowhide split in a dark wine-brown color. The vest is unlined as the leather used is heavy and unlikely to stretch.

This article required about twenty square feet of material. The basic pattern used is Simplicity's number 9087. However, several basic alterations were made before cutting or sewing began.

To check the size and length of the pattern, it was first measured against a sweater. It was then shortened two inches as a matter of personal preference. The pockets indicated in the original design were eliminated. In place of the seam that ran down the center of the back, two curved seams that run from the armholes to the hem were substituted for added shape.

To create these two new fitted seams, the paper pattern is cut where new seams are first drawn in; a five eighths inch seam allowance is added along the cut edge of each new piece. The back center seam allowance

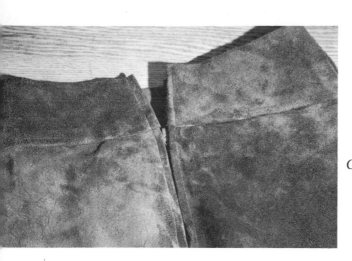

Centered application of a zipper in a skirt.

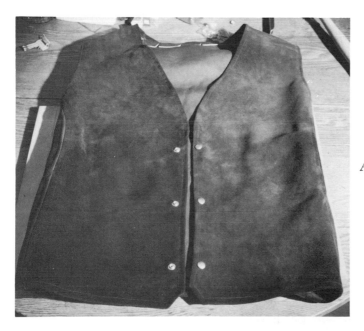

A man's vest.

*Finished curved seams
on the back of a man's vest.*

is cut off and a second piece of paper is cut to match the back and taped on to it to form one large back pattern piece with no center seam.

The same procedure should be followed to add a new seam to each side of the front of the vest.

A cloth version of the newly altered pattern can be quickly made from an old sheet to insure the fit and shape of the vest.

The pattern parts are then taped to the skins and cut out.

All seam allowances are marked on the back of the leather with a tracing wheel and chalked paper.

Sew the new seams on the front and back first. Then sew the side center seams.

To use lacing on a vest like this, follow the usual procedure and make the seam allowances one-quarter inch instead of five-eighths inch. Mark and punch holes and proceed to lace.

The seam allowances on front, neck and armhole edges are folded and cemented in place. Cut V-shaped notches on curves in the seam allowance to allow for smooth folding. These folded edges should then be top stitched one-quarter inch in from the edge.

Cement the hem in place—make it about one inch deep.

Topstitch the hem. If lacing is used, punch holes along all the folded edges.

Three snap fasteners should now be measured and set in the front of the vest. For men and boys, remember that the tops of the fasteners are on the left side and the bottom part of the fastener on the right.

HERE'S A JACKET:

Leather and suede jackets are a welcome addition to anybody's wardrobe. They're warm, durable and comfortable too. A well-made jacket will give years of service and the leathers actually seem to become more attractive as time marches on. The problems posed by setting a sleeve or turning a collar are easily surmounted by an experienced home sewer or leathercrafter—but patience, planning and care can see even a beginner through.

The jacket shown here is made of the same reversible cowhide split as the skirt previously described. The pattern used is McCall's number 2498, with a few minor variations.

148

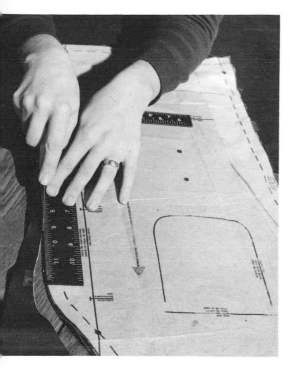

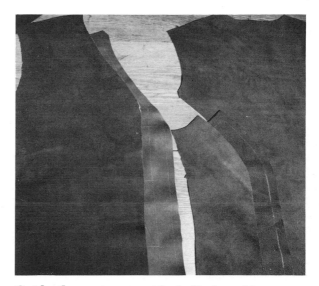

Cutting a pattern using a craft knife.

Cut leather vest parts with chalked markings on the wrong side.

For a short jacket like this one, you'll need at least twenty square feet of leather. Use the suede or lightweight leather that appeals to you. You'll also require about one and one-half yards of taffeta lining, seam binding tape, and snap fasteners—or buttons, if you prefer.

Start by choosing your pattern carefully. Several companies are now making jacket patterns specifically designed for working with leather. If you find one of these that appeals to you, it's a best bet. Otherwise, you can use patterns intended for corduroy, wool, canvas or denim. If it's the first jacket you're doing, pick a simple design that won't be too hard to work with. Bring the pattern to the leather shop with you and be sure to buy the right amount of material.

149

For your first jacket, make a muslin or old sheet version of it that's loosely stitched together. You can then make any alterations following this model. Alter your pattern parts accordingly. This may seem a tiresome step when you're anxious to get to the real thing, but it will be well worth it in the long run and can assure you a well made finished product that fits.

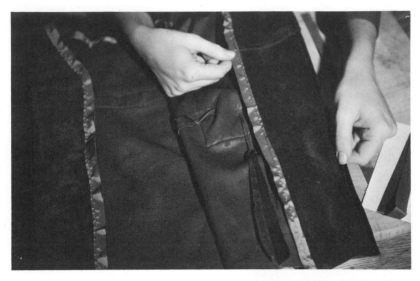

Seam binding in place on jacket facing (two views).

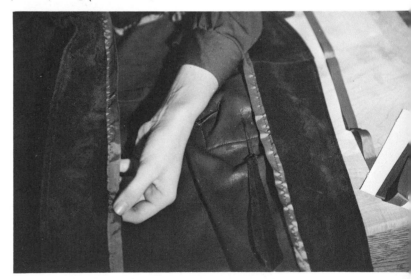

After you've made any necessary alterations to the pattern pieces, place them on the skins and cut them out. Be certain to cut a left and right sleeve and not two of the same kind. Mark seam lines and such on the wrong side of the leather with a tracing wheel and chalked paper.

Sew the body of the jacket first—follow the step by step directions included in the pattern package. Add top stitching for strength and appearance on all major seams.

You can use pins in the seam allowances to ease sewing as long as you don't pin any part of the leather that will show when the jacket is finished.

Flatten all seams with a mallet and cement them down and flatten again.

Make the collar and attach it as instructed in the pattern you're using. Leave off the waistband if there is one.

Add seam binding to the inner facing to facilitate sewing the lining in place later on.

Jacket lining sewn into sleeve and waist bands.

Lining up a sleeve to the body of a jacket.

Sew the sleeves as separate units. Sew the sleeve lining separately and then sew it into the sleeveband. Then fold the lining down into the sleeve while you fit the sleeve to the body of the jacket.

Sleeves can be a little hard to handle, so they should be pinned, taped or loosely glued in place to facilitate sewing. Attach them as follows:

Working on the inside of the jacket, pin the bottom sleeve seam to the top of the side seam of the jacket. Pin the sleeve to the jacket for about three inches on both sides of the seam. Do it so that it's smooth—with no bunching.

Now pin the center of the sleeve cap to the shoulder seam of the jacket—you'll notice that the remaining sleeve cap leather doesn't seem to fit. In fabric, this is eased, or gathered by pulling a thread—but that won't work with leather. Instead, start pinning in the seam allowance and bunch the sleeve leather around each pin; put in as many pins or use as much tape as necessary to get all of the sleeve evenly bunched around the pins and attached to the body of the jacket.

Turn the sleeve right side out to check your pinning. The sleeve

152

should appear evenly gathered and puff out a little around the shoulder seam. When it looks even, you're ready to sew.

Sew slowly once around the entire sleeve and remove the pins or tape. Now make another seam within the allowance, one-eighth inch away from the first for added strength.

Sew the body of the lining into the body of the jacket by hand. Fold the lining edges under the seam binding and sew into the seam binding.

If there's a waistband, pin it on and sew it in place and include the bottom of the lining as you sew.

Now retrieve the sleeve lining and sew it by hand to the body of the lining. Ease the extra sleeve material and turn under both edges as you sew.

You're now ready to attach the snap fasteners. In this case, there's one on each pocket, one on each sleeve band, five down the front and three on the waistband. You can vary these as you see fit, for instance by putting two on each pocket or two on the waistband, just as you like it.

Jacket sleeve and body linings, joined with the slipstitch done by hand.

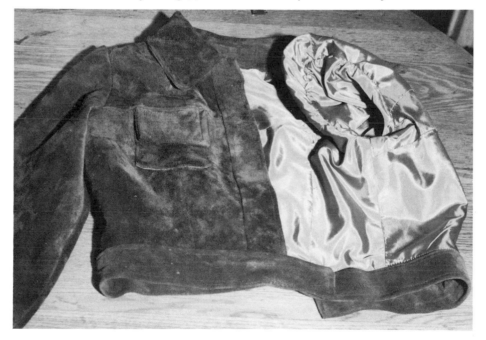

To lace a jacket, make all seam allowances one-quarter inch wide. Follow the instructions as if you were sewing as you make use of the lacing stitch of your choice. Work from the right side of the leather so that you can see how the laces look as you progress.

Use rubber cement or tape to hold seams in place as you lace. Omit the lining, as any fabric lining will fray if it is laced into the seams of the leather and a leather lining will make the jacket too bulky. Snap fasteners can be used on laced jackets and are applied in the usual way.

INDEX

158

W

Waxes, pastes and oils, 101
Wire cutter, 25
    use in leather work, 24
Writing secretary or pad holder,
    115–119
        pattern, 116–117

Y

Yard measure conversion to feet, 36
    (for patterns with yardage re-
    quirements)

Z

Zippers, 61
    for pillows, 108
    for skirts, 144, 146